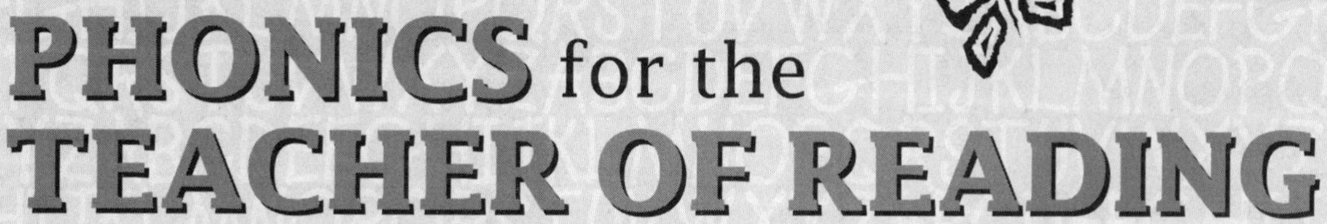

PHONICS for the TEACHER OF READING

Programmed for Self-Instruction

Eighth Edition

Barbara J. Fox
North Carolina State University

Marion A. Hull
Northern Illinois University, Emerita

Upper Saddle River, New Jersey
Columbus, Ohio

Library of Congress Cataloging-in-Publication Data

Fox, Barbara J.
Phonics for the teacher of reading : programmed for self-instruction/Barbara J. Fox, Marion A. Hull.—8th ed.
p. cm.
Hull's name appears first on the earlier edition.
ISBN 0-13-026538-1
1. Reading—Phonetic method—Programmed instruction. 2. Teaching—Aids and devices. I. Hull, Marion A. II. Title.
LB1573.3 .H85 2002
372.46'5—dc21

00-066829

Vice President and Publisher: Jeffery W. Johnston
Editor: Linda Ashe Montgomery
Production Editor: Mary M. Irvin
Design Coordinator: Diane C. Lorenzo
Project Coordination and Text Design: Carlisle Publishers Services
Cover Design: Thomas Mack
Cover Photo: Uniphoto
Production Manager: Pamela D. Bennett
Director of Marketing: Kevin Flanagan
Marketing Manager: Krista Groshong
Marketing Coordinator: Barbara Koontz

This book was set in Stone Sans by Carlisle Communications, Ltd., and was printed and bound by R.R. Donnelley & Sons Company. The cover was printed by Phoenix Color Corp.

Prentice-Hall International (UK) Limited, *London*
Prentice-Hall of Australia Pty. Limited, *Sydney*
Prentice-Hall Canada, Inc., *Toronto*
Prentice-Hall Hispanoamericana, S.A., *Mexico*
Prentice-Hall of India Private Limited, *New Delhi*
Prentice-Hall of Japan, Inc., *Tokyo*
Prentice-Hall Singapore Pte. Ltd
Editora Prentice-Hall do Brasil, Ltda., *Rio de Janeiro*

10 9 8 7 6 5 4 3
ISBN 0-13-026538-1

Preface

Reading is a complicated process. It requires competence in several sets of skills including the ability to identify and recognize words which leads to developing independence in reading. This text presents the content of phonics and its use as one set of word attack skills. It should be especially helpful to classroom teachers, reading teachers, and special education teachers. A knowledge of the content of phonics is important for teachers because the English language is based on the alphabetic principle—the principle that letters represent speech sounds—to transcribe spoken language into written language. When teachers teach phonics, they help students learn, understand, and apply the alphabetic principle to reading and spelling.

What Does the Research Say about Teaching Phonics?

In a recent analysis of American-English spelling, Venezky (1999) describes English as a fundamentally alphabetic writing system. It is not surprising, then, that researchers (Carr & Posner, 1995; Adams, 1990) conclude that reading achievement is higher when instructional programs include phonics. Classroom teachers also recognize the importance of phonics for the teaching of reading. When a national sample of kindergarten through second-grade teachers was asked to describe their perspective on phonics instruction, nearly all of them said that phonics is a significant component of their own classroom reading program (Baumann, Hoffman, Moon, & Duffy-Hester, 1998). In its report on early reading, the Committee on the Prevention of Reading Difficulties in Young Children (Snow, Burns, & Griffin, 1998), recommend that children develop a knowledge of, and the ability to use, the letter-sound associations of the English language. After analyzing the research in reading, the National Institute of Child Health and Human Development (2000) came to the conclusion that phonics, when taught systematically, significantly improves the reading ability of elementary-age children. The subgroup responsible for assessing the research in phonics instruction reports that a knowledge of phonics not only improves spelling, but it also has a positive effect on children's ability to read and comprehend text (National Institute of Child Health and Human Development, 2000).

While phonics is certainly critical for learning to read the English language, it is only one of many components in a balanced classroom reading program. The International Reading Association (1997) emphasizes this point, noting that effective phonics instruction should not only lead to independence in reading, but should also be linked to children's reading and writing. In order for you, the teacher, to instruct and support children as they learn and apply phonics to reading and spelling, you need to understand how written English uses the 26 letters of the alphabet to represent as many as 44 different speech sounds.

How Is This Text Organized?

This text, *Phonics for the Teacher of Reading,* is set up as a self-paced program of instruction that has proved to be a useful technique for presenting phonics background to readers. Thus, the text will guide you through a series of small steps to help you learn the terminology associated with phonics, develop phonics concepts, and clinch your understandings of how phonics instruction can impact children's reading ability. Brief reviews, comprehensive reviews, and a pretest and posttest will enable you to measure your growth as you follow along.

To further assist you in your study, this latest revision of the text includes 13 new study guides, arranged in tables, which give you concise overviews of the letters, key pronunciation symbols, and generalizations you are studying. For example, the study guide on onsets and rimes lists 50 frequently occurring rimes (vowel and consonant combinations in the English language). To help you apply this information when teaching, a new appendix lists all of the key English sounds and words that represent these sounds.

In addition, scattered throughout this new edition are ten boxed features that explain some of the more intriguing aspects of the history of our English writing system. These selections provide you with interesting information about the sounds of language and explain the reasons why we use certain letters and letter–sound combinations in our language today. These brief accounts will enhance your insight into, and appreciation for, our American-English spelling system.

Through reading and studying this text, you will increase your understanding of the content of phonics, and, as a consequence of this new understanding, your ability to be an effective teacher of reading.

Acknowledgments

We would like to thank the reviewers of this text. We appreciate their insightful guidance: Carol J. Fuhler, Iowa State University; Rosie Webb Joels, The University of Central Florida; Darlene M. Michener, California State University—Los Angeles; Karen Robinson, Otterbein College; and John T. Wolinski, Salisbury State University.

References

Adams, M. J. (1990). *Beginning to read: Thinking and learning about print.* Cambridge, MA: MIT Press.

Baumann, J. F., Hoffman, J. V., Moon, J., & Duffy-Hester, A. M. (1998). Where are teachers' voices in the phonics/whole language debate? Results from a survey of U.S. elementary classroom teachers. *The Reading Teacher, 51,* 636–650.

Carr, T. H., & Posner, M. I. (1995). The impact of learning to read on the functional anatomy of language processing. In B. de Gelder & J. Morais (Eds.), *Speech and reading: A comparative approach* (pp. 267–301). East Sussiz, United Kingdom: Erlbaum (UK) Taylor & Francis.

International Reading Association. (1997). *The role of phonics in reading instruction: A position statement of the International Reading Association* [Brochure]. Newark, DE: Author.

National Institute of Child Health and Human Development. (2000). *Report of the national reading panel: Teaching children to read: An evidence-based assessment of the scientific research literature on reading and its implications for reading instruction.* (NIH Publication No. 00-4769.) Washington, DC: U.S. Government Printing Office.

National Institute of Child Health and Human Development. (2000). *Report of the national reading panel: Teaching children to read: An evidence-based assessment of the scientific research literature on reading and its implications for reading instruction: Reports of the subgroups.* (NIH Publication No. 00-4769.) Washington, DC: U.S. Government Printing Office.

Snow, C. E., Burns, M. S., & Griffin, P. (1998). *Preventing reading difficulties in young children.* Washington, DC: National Academy Press.

Venezky, R. L. (1999). *The American way of spelling.* New York: The Guilford Press.

Contents

Self-evaluation I:

A Pretest

This is a test designed to give an indication of your present knowledge in the field of phonics. Read each item, including all the choices. Indicate the answer you consider best by circling the appropriate letter (a, b, c, d, or e) or marking the appropriate letter on an answer sheet. Be sure to respond to every item. Time: 30 minutes.

I. Multiple Choice. Select the best answer.

1. A requirement of a syllable is that

- **a.** it contain at least one consonant letter.
- **b.** it contain no more than one vowel letter.
- **c.** it contain no more than one vowel phoneme.
- **d.** it contain no more than one phoneme.
- **e.** All of the above

2. Which of the following most adequately completes the sentence? The consonant speech sounds in the American-English language are represented by

- **a.** the distinctive speech sounds we associate with the 21 consonant letters of the alphabet.
- **b.** 18 of the consonant letters of the alphabet plus certain digraphs.
- **c.** the single-letter consonants plus their two- and three-letter blends.
- **d.** The American-English language is too irregular to represent the consonant speech sounds with any degree of accuracy.

3. The letter *y* is most likely to be a consonant when

- **a.** it is the first letter in a word or syllable.
- **b.** it is the final letter in a word or syllable.
- **c.** it follows *o* in a syllable.
- **d.** it has the sound of *i* as in *might.*
- **e.** None of the above

4. Generally, when two like-consonants appear together in a word,
   a. only one is sounded.
   b. one is sounded with the first syllable and the other with the second.
   c. both are sounded when the preceding vowel is *i.*
   d. both are sounded when the following vowel is *e.*
   e. neither is sounded.

5. The second syllable of the nonsense word *alithpic* would be expected to rhyme with
   a. aright.
   b. brick.
   c. kith.
   d. pyth (as in python).
   e. hit.

6. The open syllable of the nonsense word *botem* would most likely rhyme with
   a. coat.
   b. hot.
   c. rah.
   d. low.
   e. gem.

bo – low

7. A diphthong is best illustrated by the vowels representing the sound of
   a. *ow* in *snow.*
   b. *ou* in *mouse.*
   c. *oo* in *foot.*
   d. *ai* in *said.*
   e. a and b

8. The sound of the schwa is represented by
   a. the *a* in *baited.*
   b. the *e* in *early.*
   c. the *e* in *happen.*
   d. the *w* in *show.*
   e. All of these

9. How many phonemes are represented in *knight?*

   a. one b. two c. three d. four e. six

10. An example of a closed syllable is
   a. desk.
   b. hot.
   c. tight.
   d. All of these
   e. None of these

11. The consonant cluster is illustrated by

a. the *sh* in *shirt.*
b. the *ng* in *thing.*
c. the *ph* in *graph.*
d. the *br* in *brought.*
e. a, c, and d

12. Which of the following has an incorrect diacritical mark?

a. căll **b.** sĕll **c.** ĭll **d.** hŏt **e.** ŭp

13. Which of the following has an incorrect diacritical mark?

a. māde **b.** sēe **c.** tīme **d.** lōve **e.** ūse

14. When the single vowel *i* in an accented syllable is followed by a single consonant and a final *e,* the *i* would most likely have the sound of

a. the *i* in *active.*
b. the *y* in *my.*
c. the *i* in *easily.*
d. the first *e* in *bee.*
e. None of the above

15. If *o* were the only and final vowel in an accented syllable, that *o* would most likely represent the same sound as

a. the *o* in *nothing.*
b. the *a* in *wanted.*
c. the *o* in *do.*
d. the *ew* in *sew.*
e. None of these

16. The letter *q* could be removed from the alphabet because it could adequately and without conflict be represented by

a. the "soft sound of *c.*"
b. *ch* as in *chair.*
c. *k* as in *keep.*
d. All of the above
e. The idea is foolish; *qu* represents a distinctive consonant sound.

17. If *a* were the single vowel in an accented syllable ending with one or more consonants, that *a* would most likely represent the same sound as

a. the *ai* in *plaid.*
b. the *ay* in *ray.*
c. the *a* in *all.*
d. the *a* in *any.*
e. None of these

18. When *oa* appear together in a syllable, they usually represent the same sound as

a. the *o* in *bottle.*
b. the *o* in *labor.*
c. the *o* in *toil.*
d. the *o* in *come.*
e. None of these

19. The symbol *s* is used in the dictionary to show the pronunciation of the sound heard in

a. shall **b.** his **c.** sugar **d.** seem **e.** b and d

20. If *e* were the only vowel in an open syllable, the *e* would most likely represent the same sound as

a. the *e* in *pine.*
b. the *ea* in *meat.*
c. the *y* in *my.*
d. the *e* in *set.*
e. None of these

21. The word *if* ends with the same sound as

a. the *ph* in *graph.*
b. the *f* in *of.*
c. the *gh* in *taught.*
d. the *gh* in *ghetto.*
e. a and b

22. The letter *c* followed by *i* is most likely to represent the same sound as

a. the *s* in *sent.*
b. the *c* in *cello.*
c. *c* followed by *o.*
d. *c* followed by *e.*
e. Both a and d

23. The letter *g* followed by *o* is most likely to represent the same sound as

a. the *j* in *joke.*
b. the *g* in *ghost.*
c. the *g* in *swing.*
d. *g* followed by *e.*
e. Both a and d

II. Multiple Choice. Where does the accent fall in the words or nonsense words given at the left? Indicate your answer by selecting the last two letters of the accented syllable found in the same row as the word.

Look at the example: *showboat.* The first "word" in a compound word is generally accented: *show′boat.* Look for the last two letters of *show, ow,* in the row to the right. You would circle b or mark b on your answer sheet.

Example:

showboat **a.** ho (**b.**) ow **c.** bo **d.** at

24. contract (noun) **a.** co **b.** on **c.** nt **d.** ra **e.** ct

25. frottomly **a.** ro **b.** ot **c.** to **d.** om **e.** ly

26. plargain **a.** la **b.** ar **c.** rg **d.** ga **e.** in

27. desridly **a.** de **b.** es **c.** ri **d.** id **e.** ly

28. cidaltion **a.** ci **b.** id **c.** da **d.** al **e.** on

29. phight **a.** hi **b.** ig **c.** gh **d.** ht

III. Complete each sentence by selecting the word for which the correct pronunciation is indicated.

30. I went to the park for a

a. pĭc′nĭc **b.** wôk **c.** rəst **d.** păr′tē **e.** rĭde

31. When I picked my vegetables, I dropped a

a. lĕt′ĭs lēv **b.** kūk′ŭm bər **c.** kăr′ŏt **d.** kăb′ĭg **e.** bēt

32. The tree we planted was a

a. pälm **b.** wĭl′ou **c.** māp′le **d.** kŏt′ ən wŭd **e.** sĭk′ə môr

33. I went to the men's store to get (a)

a. sŏgz **b.** shōōz **c.** trou′sərs **d.** chərt **e.** nək′ tī′

34. The wall is

a. krăkt **b.** smōōth **c.** rôf **d.** pānt əd′ **e.** t̸hĭk

35. The comittee was composed of

a. klûr′ gĭ mĕn **b.** bo͝ok mĭn′ **c.** băngk′ ərz **d.** tē zhərs **e.** jŭd′jĭs

IV. Multiple Choice. Select the word in each row that is incorrectly syllabicated.

36. **a.** ro bot **b.** ro bin **c.** ro bust **d.** ro tor **e.** rouge

37. **a.** let hal **b.** rab bit **c.** dras tic **d.** mer cy **e.** con nect

38. **a.** un der line **b.** un e qual **c.** un ite **d.** pre dic a ment **e.** re mit

39. **a.** home work **b.** book man **c.** eye ball **d.** now here **e.** egg nog

V. Multiple Choice. There are three "words" in each item (a, b, c). Select the word in which you would hear the same sound as that represented by the underlined part of the word at the left. You may find that the sound is heard in all three words; if so, mark d. If none of the words contain the sound, mark e.

40. mention	**a.** special	**b.** sugar	**c.** machine	**d.** All	**e.** None
41. the	**a.** thistle	**b.** mother	**c.** think	**d.** All	**e.** None
42. jet	**a.** gnome	**b.** gentle	**c.** sang	**d.** All	**e.** None
43. into	**a.** thick	**b.** watch	**c.** hoped	**d.** All	**e.** None
44. success	**a.** cheese	**b.** knee	**c.** queer	**d.** All	**e.** None
45. home	**a.** honor	**b.** night	**c.** who	**d.** All	**e.** None
46. tall	**a.** talk	**b.** fault	**c.** gnaw	**d.** All	**e.** None
47. food	**a.** look	**b.** blood	**c.** bought	**d.** All	**e.** None
48. boil	**a.** mouse	**b.** employ	**c.** riot	**d.** All	**e.** None
49. would	**a.** whom	**b.** once	**c.** cow	**d.** All	**e.** None
50. sang	**a.** ranger	**b.** ponder	**c.** thinker	**d.** All	**e.** None

VI. Multiple Choice. Select the letter(s) at the right that represents the onset in each one-syllable word.

51. splurge	**a.** sp	**b.** ge	**c.** lur	**d.** spl	**e.** urge
52. cherry	**a.** ch	**b.** erry	**c.** her	**d.** cher	**e.** erry
53. throw	**a.** thr	**b.** ro	**c.** ow	**d.** th	**e.** row
54. fluid	**a.** uid	**b.** id	**c.** lui	**d.** fl	**e.** flu
55. roast	**a.** roa	**b.** oa	**c.** st	**d.** oast	**e.** r

VII. Multiple Choice. Select the letter(s) at the right that represents the rime in each one-syllable word.

56. steam	**a.** ea	**b.** eam	**c.** st	**d.** team	**e.** ste
57. rhyme	**a.** rh	**b.** yme	**c.** rhy	**d.** hyme	**e.** rhy
58. catch	**a.** atch	**b.** tch	**c.** cat	**d.** ch	**e.** at
59. school	**a.** ch	**b.** choo	**c.** ool	**d.** hool	**e.** sch
60. dress	**a.** ess	**b.** dr	**c.** dre	**d.** ress	**e.** re

(see p. 202 for answers to Self-evaluation I.)

Number correct ________________

Part I

General Knowledge and Terminology

What kind of background do you have in phonics needed for teaching children to read? To help determine the depth of your present knowledge or lack of knowledge and to aid in evaluating your growth, this text includes a pretest and a posttest. Do not examine the posttest now. You may wish to remove the posttest and file it away, awaiting the completion of your study of this programmed text.

Turn to page 1 and take the pretest now. Correct it. At your next sitting, turn back to this section and continue reading.

Now that you have completed the pretest, you are ready to continue with this program.

Phonics and Reading

Our spoken language is a sound system by which we communicate with one another. Written language is the system of symbols used to represent the sounds of our spoken language. Readers study phonics so that they can translate the written symbols—the letters of the English alphabet—into the sounds which make up the words of spoken English. Therefore, in order for phonics to be an effective tool for word identification, readers must already have in their speaking vocabularies the words that they pronounce with the use of phonics.

A mutually beneficial relationship exists between the opportunity to use phonics knowledge in reading and the opportunity to use phonics knowledge in spelling. When children write, they analyze the letter-sound relationships in the words they do not know how to spell. This analysis helps children develop insight into the way that letters represent sounds in words. The more children know about the letter and sound associations of phonics, the greater the likelihood that as readers they will be able to use phonics to identify visually unfamiliar words in text.

The teaching of phonics involves five approaches: (1) Phonics can be taught with a direct instruction approach in which the children learn the letter patterns of the English language in a prescribed sequence. This approach, which is also called synthetic phonics, requires that the children learn the sounds represented by letter patterns, and then blend the sounds so as to pronounce meaningful words. (2) Phonics can be taught through spelling. In the spelling approach, children are taught to separate the words they wish to spell into sounds (called phonemes), and then to select the letters that represent those sounds. (3) Children can be taught to analyze the words their teachers have already taught—known words—into letter and sound components. In using this approach, called analytic phonics, the children consider the patterns of letters and sounds within the context of familiar, whole words. (4) Another approach is to embed phonics instruction in ongoing textual reading. This approach tends to be more implicit, and typically does not include a specified learning scope and sequence. Here, the letter-sound patterns the children learn are the associations that they need to know to identify the words in the books they are reading and to spell words on their own when writing. (5) Phonics can be taught by showing children how to make analogies from known words to unknown words. In the analogy approach, the children use the familiar patterns in known words to unlock the pronunciation of unknown words that share the same letter-sound patterns.

Whether phonics is taught with a direct (synthetic), spelling, analytic, embedded, or analogy approach, it is an important source of information for unlocking the identity of words that readers do not automatically recognize. Phonics, however, is not the only source of important information available to readers. Often, readers combine their knowledge of phonics with other sources of information to determine the identity of unknown words.

Although success in the use of phonics depends on a knowledge of the letter and sound associations of our English writing system and on the ability to use this knowledge in combination with other sources of information, it also depends on a special type of language understanding which we call phonological awareness. Phonological awareness is the conscious knowledge that spoken words are made up of individual sounds, and that individual speech sounds can be combined to form meaningful words. You will learn more about this and other topics when you respond to the self-teaching material that follows. Before you turn to this material, read the next section, which explains how this book is designed to help you develop the knowledge of phonics you need to teach reading.

How to Use This Book

Read these directions carefully. The success of your study depends chiefly on two factors: (1) your desire to obtain a background in phonics to aid you in teaching children to read; and (2) the care with which you follow the directions as you proceed through this program.

The program is arranged in frames. Each frame requires a response. The left portion of the frame indicates the expected response. It is absolutely essential that you write your response *before* you see this expected response. To avoid glancing at the left column, cut the mask from the back cover of this book or make one of heavy paper. Place the mask over the left-hand column to conceal the correct response.

When you have studied and written your response to the first frame, move the mask down to reveal the answer to that frame. Compare your answer with the expected answer. Since this is a teaching device (not a test) and is designed to guide you to the correct response, you will more than likely find that you have the correct answer. If you do not, study the material again. Write the correct response. Equivalent answers may be considered correct; make sure that they are equivalent.

You will find that there is much repetition and review. This will help you fix the important points in your mind. It may seem that you are asked to make simple, obvious answers. You may be tempted not to write them and instead to respond mentally or look at the answers while you are reading the frame. *THIS WILL DEFEAT THE PURPOSE OF THE PROGRAM* and will be a waste of your time. It is essential that you make the written response or responses to the entire frame before you see the answers.

Do not work too long at one sitting. Several periods in one day will prove to be better than one long period. Arrange your study so that you will be able to keep an active mind.

Now cover the left-hand column below. Study the first frame. Make the required response. (In this case you will select the correct word from the two choices under the blank.) Move the mask down to reveal the answer to the first frame. Compare the two so that your learning is immediately reinforced. If your answer is correct, study the second frame. Fill in the blank. If you read the first frames with an active mind, you will make the correct answers. If you are incorrect, review; then write the correct answers. Proceed through the following frames in a similar fashion.

spoken	**1.** The language of any people is the sound system by which the individuals communicate with one another. The written language is merely a system of symbols, a code, used to represent the ______ language. (written, spoken)
code (or symbols)	**2.** Therefore, one of the basic steps in the reading process is **decoding:** translating the ______ into the sounds of the spoken language.
symbols (or code)	**3.** We study phonics to learn the code so that we can translate the written ______ into the spoken sounds. But, to our regret, the code is not perfect; part of our study involves its inconsistencies. We shall begin our study by examining the basic elements of the code, the **phoneme** and the **grapheme**.

phoneme	**phoneme** **grapheme** **4.** The suffix *eme* denotes a basic structural element of a language. *Phon* (telephone, phonograph, etc.) refers to voice or sound. One speech sound is called a ____________ (*phon* + *eme*).
sound	**5.** These word-pairs illustrate the definition of a phoneme. As you pronounce each pair, notice the sound that makes the top word different from the one beneath it. *pin* *pin* *pin* *pin* *tin* *pen* *pit* *chin* **A phoneme is the smallest unit of ____________ that distinguishes one word from another.**
t	**6.** To attain a better understanding of a phoneme, let us examine these words more closely. How does *pin* differ from *tin?* *pin* *tin* The sounds represented by the *p* and the ____________ are the smallest units of sound that distinguish *pin* from *tin.*
sound *i, e*	**7.** Compare the phonemes represented by the underlined letters in the set of words at the right. *pin* *pen* Remember that the phoneme is a ____________ , so say the words aloud. The sounds that are represented by the _____ and the _____ are the smallest units that distinguish *pin* from *pen.*
n, t	**8.** Pronounce the words at the right. The sounds that are represented by the _____ and the _____ are the smallest units that distinguish *pin* from *pit.* *pin* *pit*
/r/ */p/*	**9.** We can hear sounds, but we cannot write sounds. For example, we cannot write the sound of l. We can say, "the sound represented by l," or "the phoneme recorded by l." There is also a symbol, / /, which indicates that we are referring to the phoneme of the specific letter or letters enclosed with slashes: /l/. How will we write symbolically the phoneme we associate with the letter *r?* ______ The phoneme represented by the key symbol *p?* _____ **The symbol /*b*/ refers to the phoneme represented by the key symbol *b*.**

BOX 1.1

Green Glass or Green Grass?

Two English Phonemes

Use your knowledge of the phonemes in the English language to answer the three questions below. Read each question aloud, and write the answer on the line.

1. The second phoneme in *glass* and the second phoneme in *grass* are ________________ .
   (the same, different)

2. The first phoneme in *late* is ________________ the first phoneme in *rate.*
   (the same as, different from)

3. *Fire* and *file* are ________________ English words.
   (the same, different)

The /*r*/ and /*l*/ phonemes (here presented between two slashes) are distinctly different in the English language. Therefore, you hear two separate phonemes and, by extension, two different words when you pronounce *glass* and *grass.* These phonemes, which are entirely distinct to you, a fluent speaker of the English language, are not so distinct and so simple to differentiate for native speakers of the Japanese language.

The Japanese language does not have an equivalent phoneme for the English /*r*/. Because the Japanese *r* is a combination of the English /*r*/ and /*l*/, speakers of Japanese may perceive the /*l*/ and the /*r*/ as variations of the same phoneme. Not only do speakers of the Japanese language have difficulty in distinguishing the English language /*r*/ from the /*l*/, but they may well confuse these two phonemes when pronouncing English words, perhaps saying "grass" when the intended word is "glass."

We listen for and perceive those phonemic differences and similarities which are particular to the language that we speak. Not all languages share exactly the same phonemes, however. Children bring to your classroom, and to the speaking, reading, and writing of the English language, an awareness of the phonemes in their home, or native, languages. You can, therefore, anticipate that some children who speak Japanese as their first language may occasionally confuse the /*r*/ and /*l*/ when pronouncing, reading, and spelling English words. When children who learn to speak English as a second language have opportunities to hear, speak, read, and write English in your classroom, they develop greater sensitivity to the English language sound structure and, in so doing, create mental categories for those English phonemes that differ from the phonemes in their native language.

allophone	**allophone** **10.** *Allo(o)* denotes a variant form (allegory, parallel). We have learned that *phon* refers to the voice or sound (phoneme, telephone). A variant form of the same phoneme is called an ____________ (*allo* + *phone*).
no allophones /b/	**11.** Pronounce the words at the right. Listen carefully to the sound represented by the underlined letter. Do you hear precisely the same sound in each word? ____________ (yes, no) The slight variations in pronunciation are called ____________ . How would you symbolically represent the phoneme? ______ bee, brown, lab, blue, tub
phoneme	**12.** The first sound in *pin,* the second sound in *spin,* and the last sound in *stop* are allophones. Even though we pronounce the allophones differently, we treat them as the same ____________ .
allophones phonemes	**13.** Let us review what we have learned about allophones and phonemes. Allophones are variant forms of a single phoneme. The sounds represented by the underlined letters in the first set of words are ____________ . (bag, brag) The underlined letters in the second set of words represent two different ____________ . It is the phonemes that are important for learning phonics. (bat, pat)
grapheme	**14.** Sounds cannot be written! Letters do not speak! We use a letter or letters to represent a phoneme. *Graph* means "drawn, written, recorded." The ____________ (*graph* + *eme*) is the written representation of the phoneme. It is the unit in the written code.
p i n *p i n*	**15.** When you say the word *pin,* you hear three phonemes. We represent these three phonemes with the letters ______ ______ ______ . Put another way, the three graphemes in *pin* are ______ ______ ______ . **The grapheme is the written representation of the phoneme. As the phoneme is the unit in the sound system, the grapheme is the unit in the written code.**

BOX 1.2

An Allophone Adventure

In frames 10, 11, and 12, you learned that allophones are naturally occurring variations in the phonemes of the English language. You know that, if you listen carefully, you can hear these slight variations. For example, you can identify variations in /*b*/ as it is pronounced in the words *brick, crab,* and *blank*. But can you also feel the difference when you pronounce some allophones? Try this to find out.

1. Put your hand in front of your mouth, palm toward your face and fingers near your lips.
2. Say "pin." Notice that you feel a puff of air when pronouncing the /*p*/ in *pin*. Phonemes that produce a puff of air are called aspirated.
3. Say "spin." Notice that you do not feel a puff of air when pronouncing the /p/ in *spin*. Phonemes that do not produce a puff of air are called unaspirated. When /p/ follows /s/ in English words, /p/ is unaspirated *(spoon, speed)*.

Although the /*p*/ in *pin* is aspirated and the /*p*/ in *spin* is unaspirated, we treat them as the same sound because each is an allophone of the same English phoneme, the /*p*/.

You have now demonstrated, through this experiment, that the aspirated and unaspirated allophones of /*p*/ can, indeed, be both heard and felt.

phonemes one	**16.** Reread frame 5. We used word-pairs to illustrate the definition of a phoneme. When you said the word *chin,* you heard three ______________ . *Ch* represents one unit of sound; you cannot divide it. Since the grapheme is the written representation of the phoneme, *ch* is ______________ grapheme(s). (How many?) *pin* *chin*
ch i n *ch*	**17.** We represent the three phonemes in *chin* with the graphemes ______ ______ ______ . The sounds represented by the *p* and the _____ are the smallest units of sound that distinguish *pin* from *chin.*
ch	**18.** We represent the first phoneme in the word *chart* with the grapheme ______ .
phoneme	**19.** A grapheme is the written symbol of the ______________ . It may be composed of one or more letters.

grapheme phoneme graphemes *k, c, q*	**20.** The phoneme is a speech sound. The _____________ is composed of the symbols we use to picture the sound on paper. Say the words at the right. In each one you will hear the _____________ that we commonly associate with the underlined letter. *keep* *come* *quit* Three different _____________ are used to represent this phoneme. They are ______ , ______ , and ______ .
   three, three *w,* *a, sh* *sh*	**21.** Grapheme and letter are not synonymous. A grapheme never consists of less than a letter, but it may consist of more than one letter. The grapheme represents the phoneme. Examine the word *wash.* *w a sh* Say it aloud. It is consists of ______ phonemes. Therefore, it consists of ______ graphemes—one grapheme to represent each phoneme. The graphemes are ______ , ______ , and ______ . What letters comprise the final grapheme of the word *wash?* ______
graphemes, phonemes phoneme	**22.** We have learned that when readers decode they translate the _____________ of a written word into the _____________ of a spoken word. To be successful at decoding, readers must have a knowledge of phonics. Readers must also know that spoken language is constructed of various units, the smallest of which is the _____________ .
  phonemes	**23.** **Phonological awareness** is the understanding that spoken language is made up of words, syllables, and phonemes. It is also the understanding that individual phonemes, when blended together, form meaningful words. Therefore, readers who are phonologically aware know that spoken words are constructed of individual _____________ .

phonemes words	**24.** Reread the definition in the previous frame. You will see that phonological awareness consists of two understandings: 1. The understanding that spoken words are composed of ______________ . 2. The understanding that phonemes, when blended together, form recognizable ______________ .
three four segment (or separate)	**25.** Let us consider the first understanding. Readers who are aware of the individual phonemes in spoken words can segment, or separate, words into phonemes. Pronounce the word *tip* aloud. *Tip* is composed of _______ phonemes. (How many?) Say the word *trip. Trip* is composed of _____________ phonemes. (How many?) When you count the phonemes in a word, you _____________ the word into individual phonemes.
four three, six	**26.** Now try *meadow, cough,* and *spigot.* (Do not be misled by the number of letters in a word's spelling!) The word *meadow* consists of _____________ phonemes, *cough* of (How many?) _____________ phonemes, and *spigot* of _____________ phonemes. (How many?) (How many?)
/p/ /i/ /n/ segment	**27.** Say the word *pin* aloud. *Pin* begins with the phoneme _____________ . The phoneme in the middle of *pin* is _____________ . *Pin* ends with the phoneme _____________ . You have demonstrated the ability to _____________ the word *pin* into phonemes. (segment, blend)
/p/, /a/, /n/ /m/, /i/, /l/, /k/ /s/, /e/, /n/, /s/	**28.** Segment the following words by saying them aloud and then writing each phoneme enclosed with a slash. The word *pan* consists of the phonemes ______ , ______ , and ______ . *Milk* consists of the phonemes ______ , ______ , ______ , and ______ . *Sense* consists of the phonemes ______ , ______ , ______ , and ______ .

phoneme phonemes	**29.** Our alphabet transcribes speech at the level of the __________ . Therefore, readers of our English language must be able to segment or separate spoken words into __________ .
count note the position of	**30.** Review frames 25 through 28. In frames 25 and 26, you were asked to ______________ the phonemes in a word. (count, note the position of) Frame 27 required that you ______________ the phonemes (count, note the position of) by identifying the beginning, middle, and last phonemes in a word. Frame 28 asked you to pronounce the phonemes one-by-one.
     table *bikes* *mall* *bit*	**31.** We will now consider three activities that the teacher of reading may use to develop and demonstrate phonological awareness in the beginning reader. Let us begin with phoneme addition. In phoneme addition, the reader attaches one or more phonemes to a word or word part. Use your awareness of the phonemes of the English language to complete the phoneme addition activities below. Combine the phonemes to pronounce a word. Write the new word on the line beside each activity. A. Add /*t*/ to /*able*/. The new word is __________ . B. Add /*s*/ to the end of /*bike*/. The new word is __________ . C. Add /*m*/ to /*all*/. The new word is __________ . D. Add /*b*/ to /*it*/. The new word is __________ .
   at *top* *car* *bee*	**32.** Phoneme deletion, the second activity we will examine, is defined as removing one or more phonemes from a word. Complete the phoneme deletion activities below. Write the new word on the line beside each activity. A. Say /*flat*/. Delete the /*fl*/ from /*flat*/. The new word is __________ . B. Say /*stop*/. Delete the /*s*/ from /*stop*/. The new word is __________ . C. Say /*card*/. Delete the /*d*/ from /*card*/. The new word is __________ . D. Say /*beet*/. Delete the /*t*/ from /*beet*/. The new word is __________ .

	33. Phoneme substitution, the third activity we will consider, requires that the reader delete one or more phonemes from a word (or word part) and replace them with one or more different phonemes. Complete the phoneme substitution activities below. Write the new word on the line beside each activity.
sad	A. Say /*sat*/. Substitute /*d*/ for /*t*/ in /*sat*/. The new word is ________ .
send	B. Say /*mend*/. Substitute /*s*/ for /*m*/ in /*mend*/. The new word is ____ .
ship	C. Say /*shop*/. Substitute /*i*/ for /*o*/ in /*shop*/. The new word is _______ .
pig	D. Say /*big*/. Substitute /*p*/ for /*b*/ in /*big*/. The new word is _______ .
	34. We have studied three activities that the teacher of reading may use to develop or demonstrate phonological awareness in the beginning reader. These activities ask the reader to consciously and intentionally add, delete, or substitute phonemes. Read the descriptions below. Write the name of the activity on the line beside the description. Read all of the descriptions before answering!
deletion	A. Removing the /*s*/ from /*sat*/ to form the new word /*at*/ is an example of phoneme ____________ .
addition	B. Attaching /*b*/ to /*at*/ to pronounce the new word /*bat*/ is an example of phoneme ____________ .
substitution	C. Exchanging /*h*/ for /*f*/ in /*fat*/ to pronounce the new word /*hat*/ is an example of phoneme ____________ .
blend	**35.** We will now turn our attention to the second aspect of phonological awareness: the ability to ____________ individual phonemes into meaningful spoken words.
	36. Use your knowledge of phonics to say the phoneme represented by each grapheme in the word **laf.**
/*l*/	The grapheme **l** represents the phoneme ____________ .
/*a*/	The grapheme **a** represents the phoneme ____________ .
/*f*/	The grapheme **f** represents the phoneme ____________ .
no	You have now pronounced each phoneme in isolation. Have you pronounced a word? ____________

blend	**37.** To identify the spoken word which the graphemes in the word **laf** represent, you must associate a phoneme with each grapheme, and then you must ______________ the phonemes together.
laugh	**38.** Now blend the phonemes together. Say the phonemes aloud as you blend. The phonemes /*l*/ + /*a*/ + /*f*/ form a word you recognize in speech. Write the word the way that you would normally spell it. ______________
decoding	**39.** Sometimes blending is described as "folding sounds together." The reader blends, or folds, the phonemes together so that they form a whole spoken word. Blending is an essential aspect of ______________ .
	Try blending the phonemes below. Write the word the way that it is normally spelled.
cat	/*k*/ + /*a*/ + /*t*/ =______________
lamp	/*l*/ + /*a*/ + /*m*/ + /*p*/ =______________
tent	/*t*/ + /*e*/ + /*n*/ + /*t*/ =______________
gem	/*j*/ + /*e*/ + /*m*/ =______________
phonological awareness phonemes, blend	**40.** We have learned that readers who are successful at using phonics to decode words have developed ______________ . These readers can segment words into their individual ______________ , and can ______________ individual phonemes to pronounce the words we use in everyday conversation.
phonemes (or speech sounds)	**41.** Although there are hundreds of different speech sounds (consider the variations due to dialect, individual speech patterns, change in stress, etc.), for all practical purposes in the task of teaching reading, **we can consider the American-English language to contain 44 separate** ______________ **.**

phoneme, letter	**42.** If the code were consistent (that is, if we had one letter for each ____________ and one phoneme for each ____________), the task of teaching children to read would be much simpler than it now is.
26 phonemes	**43.** The truth is that we have only ____________ letters in our alphabet, only 26 symbols to represent 44 ____________ .
phonemes	**44.** We add symbols to our system by using combinations of letters (such as *ch, th*) to represent the ____________ not represented by the 26 letters of the alphabet.
phoneme, *a*	**45.** We also add symbols by using one letter to represent more than one _____ . (The letter _____ , for example, represents three different phonemes in the three words *ate, pan, all.*)
gh, ph phoneme	**46.** Besides lacking a one-to-one correspondence between the letters of the alphabet and the phonemes needed, the spelling of the English language is further complicated by its many inconsistencies. One of the greatest of these is the use of different symbols to represent the same phoneme. For example, the sound we associate with *f* is represented by *f* in *fine,* by _____ in *cough,* and by _____ in *elephant.* This is an example of three graphemes representing one ____________ .
k, g, h	**47.** Another of the many complications is the use of symbols that do not represent any sound: *knight* has three letters that do not represent sound; the _____ , _____ , and _____ .
letter (or symbol or grapheme)	**48.** Sometimes when a letter represents more than one phoneme, there are clues within the word to indicate which sound the ____________ represents. These clues are called graphophonic cues.
graphophonic	**49. Graphophonic cues** consist of the 26 letters (graphemes), the 44 sounds (phonemes), and the system of relationships among letters and sounds (phonics). Readers use ____________ (*grapho* + *phonic*) cues to translate the written code into the sounds of spoken language.

BOX 1.3

Spanish Phonemes

Different languages use different phonemes and different graphemes. Let us consider four Spanish phonemes that do not have an exact English language equivalent, and the graphemes that represent them.

1. The Spanish *ñ* is pronounced like the *ny* in the English word *canyon,* and is represented by the grapheme *ñ.* We hear this phoneme in the Spanish loan words *El Niño* and *La Niña.*
2. The Spanish trilled *r* is pronounced by rolling the *r* on the upper palate. A single *r* is the grapheme that indicates a slightly trilled pronunciation; a double *rr* represents a strongly trilled pronunciation. The Spanish word for dog, *perro,* is pronounced with a strongly trilled *rr.*
3. In Latin America, the *ll* is the grapheme that represents the sound of the *y* in *yellow.* In Spain, the *ll* is pronounced like the *lli* in *million. Tortilla,* a cornmeal, flat bread used in tacos and other dishes, is an example of a Spanish loan word in which the *ll* is pronounced like the *y* in *yellow* or the *lli* in million.
4. The Spanish *j* is pronounced like the English */h/* in *happy,* only farther back in the throat and with more emphasis. *Javelina,* the wild pig of the southwestern United States, is an example of a Spanish loan word in which the letter *j* represents */h/.*

The native speaker of English who wishes to speak the Spanish language must learn to pronounce the four Spanish phonemes that are not among the 44 American-English phonemes. The best way to do this is to speak Spanish, and to listen to Spanish as it is being spoken. Similarly, Spanish-speaking children who learn English as a second language benefit from many and varied opportunities to speak and listen to English, to participate in English conversations, and to hear English books read aloud.

Answers	Frame
	50. Pronounce the words at the right. You will notice that the letter *e* represents two different phonemes in these words. Graphophonic cues indicate that the letter *e* in *bed* represents the same sound as the (*ten teen / fed feed / met meet*)
ten	*e* in ____________ (*ten, teen*), and that the letter *e* in *keep* represents the same
teen	sound as the *e* in ____________ (*ten, teen*).

syntactic	**51.** Besides graphophonic cues, readers use **syntactic cues** and **semantic cues** to determine the identity of words. Syntax is the manner in which words are ordered to form phrases, clauses, and sentences. Therefore, readers who use ______________ clues recognize the manner in which word order and grammatical function are clues to the identity of a word.
hit syntactic	**52.** Consider the word order and grammatical function to determine the missing word in this sentence: The batter ______________ the ball to the right fielder. You know to choose a word that is a verb because English syntax requires the use of an action word in the structure of this sentence. When you decide that the missing word is a verb, you use ______________ cues. (graphophonic, syntactic)
semantic	**53. Semantic** refers to the meaning of language. Therefore, the meaning of a passage provides readers with ______________ cues.
semantic	**54.** Consider once again the word omitted from the sentence in frame 52. To determine that the missing word is *hit,* you must combine a background knowledge of baseball with an understanding of the meaning of this sentence. This is an example of the use of ______________ cues. (syntactic, semantic)
truck Semantic *truck*	**55.** Now read the following sentence: The dog barked at the red and blue ______________ . (*truck, tree*) ______________ cues within the sentence indicate that the missing (syntactic, semantic) word is ______________ .
graphophonic cues syntactic cues semantic cues	**56.** The three types of cues used to identify unfamiliar words are: ______________ which consist of letter and sound relationships. ______________ which consist of grammatical relationships. ______________ which consist of meaningful relationships.

	57. Readers frequently combine the information from graphophonic, syntactic, and semantic cues to determine the identity of words.
graphophonic	Readers use ______________ cues to translate the written code into (graphophonic, semantic) speech sounds.
syntactic	Readers use ______________ cues to identify words that are consistent (syntactic, semantic) with grammatical order and function.
semantic sense	Readers use ______________ cues to identify words that make (semantic, graphophonic) ______________ in a sentence.
graphophonic syntactic semantic	**58.** You have learned that readers use ______________ cues to determine the pronunciation of words they do not recognize. However, the process of word identification is strengthened when graphophonic cues are used in combination with ______________ cues and ______________ cues.
phonemes sound (or phoneme)	**59.** We have noted that the alphabet is a symbolic representation of our speech sounds (or ______________), that there is not a one-to-one correspondence between the symbol and the ______________ , and that there are many inconsistencies in the symbolic system. The code is far from perfect.
letters	**60.** However, there are certain symbols which are reliable and there are patterns of reliability within the inconsistencies. The teacher of reading must be aware of these. It is the purpose of this program to aid you in your understanding of one set of word recognition skills, that of phonics. We shall begin our study with the most reliable of the 26 ______________ of the alphabet, the consonants. (letters, phonemes)

The reviews should give you some indication of the effectiveness of your study and provide means for additional reviewing. Write the answers to the reviews on another sheet of paper. Correct them and analyze the results. Then recheck yourself after a few days by answering the review questions again. Keep track of your scores so that you will know where additional study and review are needed.

Review 1

Close your eyes and summarize the information contained in the first section. On another piece of paper, write the answers to this review without looking back. Complete the entire review before you check the answers.

1. In order to read, we must be able to ____________, that is, to translate the written symbols into the correct speech sounds.
2. The smallest unit of sound that distinguishes one word from another is called a ____________.
3. For all practical purposes, the American-English language contains ____________ phonemes.
   (26, 44)
4. What symbol can we use to represent the first sound we hear in the word *milk?*____________
   (Remember, we wish to refer to the sound, not the letter.)
5. The first sound in *track* and the last sound in *date* are ____________ of the phoneme /t/.
6. Phonological awareness consists of the ability to (1) ____________ words into their individual phonemes, and (2) ____________ individual phonemes together to form meaningful spoken words.
7. Separating the word *sat* into its individual phonemes /s/, /a/, and /t/ is an example of ____________.
8. Combining the three phonemes /s/ + /a/ + /t/ to pronounce the word *sat* is an example of ____________.
9. A ____________ is the written representation of a phoneme.
10. Are graphemes and letters synonymous?
11. Clues within words that indicate which phoneme a letter represents are called ____________ cues.

12. The way that words are ordered and function in sentences provides ____________ cues to word identification.

13. The meaning of a passage provides readers with ____________ cues to the identity of words.

Turn to the Answers section, page 197, and check your answers. You should have answered all the questions correctly. If you did not succeed, analyze your study procedure. Is your mind active? Are you writing all the answers? Do you complete a frame before you move the mask down? Did you summarize your learnings before you started the review? Study the appropriate parts of the Introduction again. Congratulations to those who had a perfect score! Your learning should be very profitable.

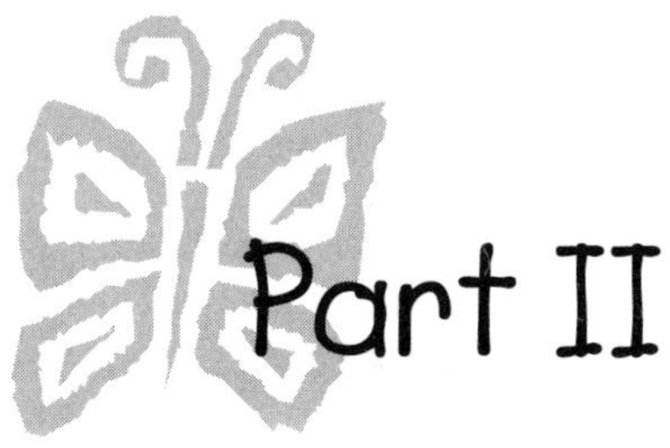

Part II

Consonants

Place the mask over the left-hand column. As you work through these sections, it will be necessary for you to make sounds out loud. Be sure that you are seated where this is possible. Now work out the first frame, move the mask down to check, and proceed as you did in the first section. Keep an active mind! You may need to study the entire frame before you make your response.

vowels	**1.** The 26 letters of the alphabet can be divided into two major categories: consonants and ______________ .
consonants	**2.** There is, however, a degree of overlapping between these categories. Certain letters, notably the *w* and *y,* sometimes function as vowels and at other times as ______________ .
consonants, 21	**3.** Recognizing the fact that we are oversimplifying the situation, we shall, in this part of the program, consider all letters except *a, e, i, o, u* to be ______________ . There are then _____ consonant letters. (How many?)
is not	**4.** We have noted previously that in the American-English language there ______________ (is, is not) a consistent one-to-one correspondence between letter and phoneme. Let us now see how this applies to consonants.

21, 25 is not	**5.** There are (for our purposes in the teaching of reading) 44 phonemes, 25 of these being consonant phonemes. There are _____ consonant letters; _____ consonant phonemes. (How many?) (How many?) There ____________ one letter for each phoneme. (is, is not)
grapheme	**6.** There are more phonemes than letters. We gain seven additional phonemes through the use of the two-letter ____________ . (grapheme, phoneme)
digraph	**7.** We call these two-letter combinations **digraphs.** Note the spelling—di for two; graph referring to writing. The two-letter combination *ch* as in *chair* is called a ____________ .
not	**8.** Pronounce the word *chair* as though each consonant were sounded. You said either "*s-hair*" or "*k-hair.*" Now pronounce *chair* as it should be pronounced. Note that you hear neither the sound represented by the *c* nor by the *h.* The combination *ch* represents a phoneme ____________ (already, not) represented by a single consonant letter. It functions like another letter of the alphabet.
c *h*	**9.** **A digraph is a two-letter combination which represents a single speech sound.** The **digraph** *ch* does not represent the sound of the _____ and the _____ with which it is spelled.
not	**10.** The phonemes of our language are very familiar to us, but to prepare ourselves to teach others to read, it is necessary to identify each of the 44 phonemes. Since there is _____ a one-to-one correspondence between sound and letter, it will be helpful to designate a key symbol for each phoneme. In this way we will know the sound to which we are referring no matter how it is represented in the word (that is, no matter how it is spelled).

yes	**11.** When possible, the key symbol will be the same as the letter we ordinarily associate with the sound. For example, *b* will serve as the key symbol for the sound we hear at the beginning of the word *box.* Would you expect *d* to serve as the key symbol for the sound heard at the beginning of the word *dog?* ___________
44 25 phonemes	**12.** There are 44 phonemes; 25 of these are consonant phonemes. We will, therefore, identify _____ key symbols altogether, of which (How many?) _____ will be consonants. (How many?) **There will be one key symbol for each phoneme. Each phoneme will have one key symbol.** There will be a one-to-one correspondence between key symbols and ___________ .
symbol letter *bomb*	**13.** Most of the consonants are reliable with respect to sound. Therefore, in most cases, the key ___________ that designates a certain phoneme heard in a word will be the same as the consonant ___________ seen in that word. For example, *b* will serve as the key symbol for the initial sound we hear in the word ___________ . (*bomb, mob*)
no (The final *b* represents no phoneme: It is a silent letter.)	**14.** Will *b* serve as the key symbol for the final sound we hear in the word *bomb?* ___________
4, 4 *g, r, a, ph* *f*	**15.** The word *graph* has _____ (How many?) phonemes and therefore _____ (How many?) graphemes. They are _____ , _____ , _____ , and _____ . So that we have a clue to its pronunciation, the logical key symbol to assign to the final phoneme in *graph* is the letter _____ .
ph *f*	**16.** Pronounce *photo.* The initial grapheme is _____ . The key symbol to represent this sound is _____ .

key symbols digraphs	**17.** We can divide the 25 consonant phonemes into two major groups: (1) Eighteen consonant phonemes identified by key symbols composed of **single letters;** and (2) Seven consonant phonemes identified by ____________ ____________ composed of **two-letter combinations** called ____________ .

Review 2

Summarize your learnings. What new words have you learned thus far? Define them.

1. Is there a one-to-one correspondence between the consonant letters and the consonant phonemes?
2. We shall learn to identify a key symbol for each of the consonant ____________ of the American-English language. (letters, phonemes)
3. The *m* is a very dependable letter; it is the key symbol for the initial sound heard in *man.* We would expect the key symbol representing the sound heard at the end of the word *jam* to be _____ .
4. Dictionaries also use _____ as the key symbol to represent the sound heard at the beginning of the word *man.*
5. Most of the key symbols will be single letters; however, seven of the consonant symbols will be composed of _____ letters called ____________ .
6. We can divide the consonant phonemes into two groups according to whether the key symbol representing the phoneme is composed of one or of two ____________ .
7. *Ch,* a ____________ , represents how many phonemes?

(For answers to the Reviews, see the Answers section, page 197.)

Single Letter Consonants

1. Place the mask firmly over the responses at the left. Do not move it until the entire frame is completed.

a. Write the 26 letters of the alphabet, in order, in the column at the right.

b. Draw a diagonal line through each of the five vowel letters.

c. Three of the 21 consonant letters do not represent distinctive sounds. Draw a horizontal line through the three unnecessary letters.

A puzzle? Clue: Say the words below, listening for the sounds that are represented by the underlined consonant letters.

city and cold

antique and quiet

exam and reflex

As single letters, *c*, *q*, and *x* do not represent distinctive phonemes.

When these words are spelled so that each consonant letter represents a distinctive phoneme, the words look like this:

sity and kold

antikue and kuiet

egzam and refleks

Eliminating the three unnecessary letters leaves us with ______________ single consonant letters which have distinctive sounds. In other words, our alphabet supplies us with ______________ single letter graphemes to represent 18 of the 25 consonant ______________ of our language.

a̸ b ~~c~~ d e̸ f g h i̸ j k l m n o̸ p ~~q~~ r s t u̸ v w ~~x~~ y z

18

18

phonemes

phonemes

3

	Key Words
b	*boat*
d	*dog*
f	*fish*
g	*goat*
h	*hat*
j	*jeep*
k	*kite*
l	*lion*
m	*moon*
n	*nut*
p	*pig*
r	*ring*
s	*sun*
t	*table*
v	*van*
w	*wagon*
y	*yo-yo*
z	*zipper*

2. As you repeat the letters of the alphabet, write the 18 consonant letters (the **key symbols**) that represent 18 distinctive ________.

You will omit the ____ consonant letters that do not represent distinctive phonemes.

How can we know exactly which phoneme has been assigned to each of the key symbols? We use a key word which has that phoneme as its initial sound. The selected key words follow, but they are out of order. Write each key word next to its key symbol.

Key Words

kite	*pig*	*van*	*boat*	*goat*	*dog*
ring	*moon*	*wagon*	*zipper*	*jeep*	*yo-yo*
sun	*lion*	*table*	*fish*	*nut*	*hat*

Key Symbols	Key Words
____	________
____	________
____	________
____	________
____	________
____	________
____	________
____	________
____	________
____	________
____	________
____	________
____	________
____	________
____	________
____	________
____	________
____	________

m	*moon*	*g*	*goat*
y	*yo-yo*	*h*	*hat*
s	*sun*	*r*	*ring*

3. Which key symbol and key word should be used to identify the initial sound heard in each of these words? Refer to frame 2 for the key words.

mat	____	________	*got*	____	________
yellow	____	________	*have*	____	________
city	____	________	*ride*	____	________

Answers	Frame
j *jeep* *f* *fish* *j* *jeep* *k* *kite* *k* *kite* *b* *boat* *g* *goat* *g* *goat*	**4.** Which key symbol and key word should be used to identify the initial sound heard in each of the following words? Use frame 2 for the key words. *jelly* ____ ________ *fat* ____ ________ *gerbil* ____ ________ *candy* ____ ________ *cat* ____ ________ *book* ____ ________ *ghost* ____ ________ *gone* ____ ________ Now check with the answers. If you missed any, say aloud the key word you selected while you listen carefully to the first phoneme. Substitute that sound in the specific study word above. Correct it so the initial sound in the study word is the same as that in the key word.
girl *gym* *goat*	**5.** Now, when we use a key symbol such as *g,* we will know that we are referring to the sound heard in ________ (*girl, gym*) and not to that heard in ________ (*girl, gym*). Check yourself. Is the phoneme you have selected the same as that heard in the key word ________ ?
key	**6.** As we study each consonant letter, we need to ask certain questions: **1.** How reliable is it? Does it always represent the sound we associate with its ________ symbol? Are there patterns of reliability? Patterns of inconsistencies? **2.** Does it have distinctive characteristics? The consonant letters have been grouped to facilitate our study in answering the above questions.

m, q, r, v

Answers	Frame
symbol *m* *m* *moon* *r* *r* *ring* *v* *v* *van*	**1.** Four of the 21 consonant letters are extremely dependable: *m, q, r,* and *v.* When we see *m, r,* or *v* in a word, we can be sure it represents the phoneme we associate with its key ______________ and is the initial sound heard in its key word. Fill in the columns at the right with the key symbols (2), and the key words (3). Select the words from the following: *van* *queen* *fish* *ring* *kite* *moon* 1 2 3 *m* _____ ______________ *r* _____ ______________ *v* _____ ______________
q *k* *kite*	*q* _____ ______________ **2.** Since *q* is an unnecessary letter, how can we call it dependable? When we see *q,* we know it represents the sound we associate with the key symbol *k.* In other words, /*q*/ = /*k*/. We can depend on it! Now write the key symbol and key word for *q* above.
k *kite*	**3.** We did not use *q* for a key symbol because the sound it represents had already been assigned to the letter _____ . We have selected one symbol to represent each of the 25 consonant sounds of our language. The key word we have selected to help identify /*k*/ is ______________ .
opak *unik* *plak* *k* *antik* *k, u, e*	**4.** Study the words at the right. The *que* combination at the end of a word represents the phoneme we associate with the key symbol _____ . Or we might say that the *q* represents the sound we associate with _____ , while the _____ and _____ are silent. *opaque* ______________ *unique* ______________ *plaque* ______________ *antique* ______________ Rewrite these words using the proper key symbol to stand for each of the consonants. Omit the silent *"ue"* combination and the silent consonants. Copy the vowels as they are, pronouncing them as they would sound in the real word.

u	**5.** The letter *q* is almost always followed by the letter _____ . In *unique,* the *u* which follows the *q* is silent.
	There are a few words that begin with *q* in which the *u* is also silent as in *quay,* or the *u* is pronounced as *u,* as in *queue.* We may miss this point because we may be mispronouncing these words. *Quay* is pronounced as though it were spelled *key; queue* is pronounced as though it were spelled *cue.*
	The first phoneme in both *key* and *cue* (therefore in *quay* and *queue*) is
k	represented by the key symbol _____ . Pronounce *quay* and *queue* correctly several times (*quay* as key; queue as *cue*). Practice reading this: *The people boarding the ship formed a queue on the quay. Three of them wore queues.*
	6. More commonly, the *u* following the letter *q* becomes a consonant and represents the sound we associate with the key symbol *w.*
	Say these words: *quilt, equal, quiet, queen, quill.* In these words the *q*
k	represents the sound we associate with _____ , and the *u* represents
w	the sound we associate with _____ .
kwick	**7.** Pronounce the words at the right aloud. Rewrite the words using the proper key symbols to show the pronunciation of the *qu* combination. *quick* ________
kwit	*quit* ________
kwiz	*quiz* ________
kween	In these words, the letter *q* represents the sound *queen* ________
k	we associate with the key symbol _____ , and the
consonant, *w*	letter *u* represents the sound of the ____________ letter _____ . (consonant, vowel)
	8. Let us summarize:
	The letters *m, q, v,* and *r* are very dependable. The *m, v,* and *r* represent distinctive sounds of their own.
k	**The *q* always represents the same sound as the _____ .**
	The letter *q* has a distinctive characteristic: It is almost always
u	followed by the letter _____ . This *u* may be silent or represent the
consonant, *w*	sound of the ______________ _____ . (consonant, vowel)

BOX 2.1

How Would a Duck Quack Without Q?

Without a sound of its own, the letter *Q* is tantamount to an alphabetical orphan in the modern English alphabet. Let us take a look at how we got this extra letter in our alphabet. The letter *Q*, known as *koppa* in the archaic Greek alphabet, fell out of use and did not survive long enough to become part of the classical Greek alphabet. We would not have the letter *Q* in our own alphabet today had not the Etruscans revived the *Q*. They passed it along to the Romans who used *Q* to spell /kw/ words (*quake, question*). Western languages inherited the Latin alphabet, although the Anglo-Saxons did not borrow this letter from Latin. The French language did borrow the Latin *Q*, however, and it was the French who added the *Q* to the English alphabet. After the Norman Conquest in 1066, French scribes began to use *Q* when spelling English words—perhaps because adding the *Q* made English words look more like French words. By sometime around 1500, the letter *Q* had become part of the English alphabet, where it remains today. If the letter *Q* were to disappear from our alphabet as it did from the classical Greek alphabet, we would use the letters *kw* and *k* in its place, depending on the sounds in the words to be spelled, such as *kwest, technik, kwiz, kwilt, opak, kwip,* and *kwit.* Consider this kwestion: If you could choose, would you discard the letter *Q* or keep it as the twenty-second letter of the English alphabet?

Ouaknin, M.C. (1999). *Mysteries of the alphabet: The origins of writing.* (J. Bacon, Trans.) New York, NY: Abbeville Press Publishers.

Review 3

1. How many phonemes are there in *panda?* How many graphemes?
2. How many phonemes are there in *chat?* How many graphemes?
3. We do not have a sufficient number of consonant letters in our alphabet to represent all the consonant sounds. Rather, we supplement the single letters with seven ______________ .
4. Which letters have not been assigned a key symbol of their own? Why?
5. To establish our code, we select key ______________ and key ___________ to represent each phoneme.
6. What key symbol represents /*m*/? _____ /*q*/? _____ /*r*/? _____ /*v*/? _____
7. *Q* is followed by _____ in English words. The *u* may be _____ as in *antique,* or have the sound of the consonant _____ as in *quilt.*
8. Using our code, how would we write the consonants in these words? *mover* ______________ *quiver* _____ .
9. What do we mean when we say, "The *v* is a very dependable letter"?

(See the Answers section for answers to Review 3.)

b, h, k, l, p

b *b* *boat* *h* *h* *hat* *k* *k* *kite* *l* *l* *lion* *p* *p* *pig*	**1.** The five consonants *b, h, k, l,* and *p* are very dependable except for the fact that on occasion they represent no phonemes. When you see one of these letters in an unknown word, you expect it to represent the sound you hear in its key word. Complete the table at the right with the letter (1), key symbol (2), and key word (3) for each. 1 2 3 ____ ____ ________ ____ ____ ________ ____ ____ ________ ____ ____ ________ ____ ____ ________ Select the key word from the following: *lion* *cat* *hat* *pig* *queen* *boat* *kite*
boat consonant	**2.** You will associate *b* with the sound heard at the beginning of the key word ____________ . Can you say that sound aloud? It is very difficult. Many consonant phonemes cannot be pronounced easily without adding a bit of the vowel sound. Some teachers, trying to pronounce the initial phoneme in *boat,* say "*buh.*" This will not help the child to identify the word *boat: buh-oat* is not *boat!* Some experts advise teachers to say "the first sound we hear in *boat*" or "the last sound we hear in *tub*" rather than to attempt to sound the phoneme in isolation. Keep in mind that it is very difficult to sound most ____________ phonemes in isolation. (consonant, vowel)
vowel	**3.** Try pronouncing /*m*/, /*v*/, /*l*/, and /*r*/. Listen to the sound you give them in *hum, dove, call,* and *car.* Say them aloud again. These are fairly easy to sound in isolation. Now say /*b*/, /*k*/, and /*p*/ aloud. Listen to them in the words *tub, back,* and *help.* Do not hang on to the sound (as you can in *hummmmmmmmm*); just softly expel your breath. Try to sound them with as little of the ____________ phoneme as possible.
silent silent	**4.** Sometimes these consonant letters have no phonemes. It is common practice to call them " ____________ letters." Certain patterns help determine whether these letters represent a phoneme or are ____________ in an unknown word.

	5. One pattern is very common to almost all consonants: **Two like-consonants appearing together in a word generally represent one phoneme.** Is this true even of the consonants we called extremely
yes	dependable? ______ .
	Say these words aloud. How many phonemes do the two like-
one	consonants represent? ____ Make a slash through the second like-consonant to depict the silent letter. Then rewrite the words omitting the silent consonant.
muf/fin, mufin, let/ter, leter, pur/r, pur	*muffin* ______ *letter* ______ *purr* ______
rib/bon, ribon, hap/pen, hapen, les/s, les	*ribbon* ______ *happen* ______ *less* ______
clim *lam* *bom* *number*	**6.** Pronounce the words at the right. Rewrite these words omitting the silent letters. (Do not be concerned with the vowel sounds at this point. We will indicate the vowel sounds later.) *climb* ______ *lamb* ______ *bomb* ______ *number* ______
b, m	The ____ is silent when it follows an ____ in the same syllable.
	7. The *b* is not silent in *number,* because it is not in the same
syllable, *m*	______ as the ____ .
	8. Pronounce the two words at the right. The *b* when *bomb*
is	followed by the *m* in *bomb* ______ silent. The *b* in is, is not
is not	*bombard* ______ silent. *bombard* is, is not
syllables	The *b* and the *m* in *bombard* are in different ______ .

dout *det* *obtain* *sutle* *t* *subtle* *t*	**9.** Pronounce the words at the right. Rewrite the words omitting the silent consonants. *doubt* _____ *debt* _____ *obtain* _____ *subtle* _____ The *b* is silent when it is followed by a _____ in the same syllable. Which word does not belong in the set? __________ Then notice that *b* is silent even though the *b* and the _____ are in different syllables.
b	**10.** Let us summarize: **When *b* follows *m* or precedes *t* in the same syllable,** **the __________ is usually silent.**
/*h*/ *hat* final	**11.** *H,* as a single letter (phoneme / /, key word __________), has a distinctive characteristic: It is never heard as the __________ sound in a word or syllable. (initial, final)
oh, hurrah, shah no	**12.** *H* is silent when it follows the vowel in a word or syllable. Put a slash through the silent *h*s in the following words: *oh* *hurrah* *shah* Check carefully. Do you hear the /*h*/ at the end of these words? __________
heir, hour, honest	**13.** The *h* may even be silent when it appears as the initial consonant of a word. There are no clues to tell us whether the initial *h* represents a phoneme. In fact, some people consider the *h* to be silent in *homage, humble, herb.* Circle the words below in which the initial *h* is silent. *here* *heir* *hour* *happy* *honest*
g, k, *r*	**14.** Study the words at the right. The letter *h* is silent when it follows the consonants _____ , _____ , and _____ . *ghost* *khaki* *rhyme* *ghastly* *khan* *rhino*

Answers	Frame	Words
gost, kaki, ryme, *gastly, kan, rino*	**15.** Rewrite the words in the preceding frame, omitting the silent consonants: __________, __________, __________, __________, __________, __________.	
khaki, ghost *rhino* *hurrah* *hour*	**16.** Review by filling in these blanks. Use the words at the right to assist you. **The letter *h* is silent when it follows the consonants *k*** (as in __________), ***g*** (as in __________), **or *r*** (as in __________). ***H* is silent when it follows a vowel** (as in __________). **Sometimes *h* is silent at the beginning of a word** (as in __________).	*hurrah* *khaki* *hour* *ghost* *rhino*
gh *laugh* *sh* *wish* *ph* *phone* *ch* *change* *wh* *white* *th* *thorn* 6 (or 5. You would not be incorrect if you omitted *wh* /*hw*/.)	**17.** Aside from the fact that *h* is often silent, as a single letter grapheme, it is reliable. However, we cannot say that whenever we see an *h* in a word we know it will either be silent or represent the initial sound heard in *hat*. *H* is a component of several digraphs (a two-letter combination which represents a single speech sound). Study the words at the right. How many digraphs contain the letter *h*, but not /*h*/? _____ Underline them.	*laugh* *wish* *phone* *change* *white* *thorn*
phoneme *kite*	**18.** Except when silent, the *k* is a very dependable letter. Let us be sure we understand: There are other graphemes which represent the sound we associate with the key symbol *k* (*queen, choir, coat*), but when we see the letter *k* in a word, we can be quite sure that when we hear the word, we will hear the same __________ as that heard at the beginning of its key word, __________.	

Answers	Frame	Words
nob *unnown* **n** *nit* *nee*	**19.** Study the words at the right to discover the "silent *k*" pattern. **The *k* is silent at the beginning of a word or syllable when followed by _____ .** Rewrite these words omitting the silent *k*s. Pronounce aloud the words you have written.	*knob* ____________ *unknown* ____________ *knit* ____________ *knee* ____________
nife *buble* *hero* *clim* *onor* *nee*	**20.** Rewrite the following words, omitting silent consonants. *knife* ____________ *bubble* ____________ *hero* ____________ *climb* ____________ *honor* ____________ *knee* ____________	
lion */l/*	**21.** The consonant *l* is another very reliable letter. To help distinguish its phoneme, we have chosen the key word ____________ . We can represent its phoneme, thus / /.	
baloon *dolar* *jely* *bel*	**22.** However, the *l* may be silent. Study the words at the right to see if this generalization applies. **Two like-consonants appearing together in a word generally represent one phoneme.** Rewrite the words omitting silent consonants.	*balloon* ____________ *dollar* ____________ *jelly* ____________ *bell* ____________
cam *(kam)* *pam* *yok* *chak* *woud* *shoud*	**23.** To discover another pattern, study the words at the right. **The letter *l* is sometimes silent when followed in the same syllable by *m*, *k*, or *d*.** Rewrite these words omitting silent consonants. (Do you hear the /l/ when you say *calm* and *palm?* If so, this is a regional difference in pronunciation, and a natural variation in the way we pronounce words.)	*calm* ____________ *palm* ____________ *yolk* ____________ *chalk* ____________ *would* ____________ *should* ____________

no	**24.** Is this a dependable pattern? ________
	Rewrite the words below omitting silent consonants.
gold *tak* *film*	*gold* ________ *talk* ________ *film* ________
milk *caf* *wak*	*milk* ________ *calf* ________ *walk* ________
	(Pronouncing the /l/ in *gold, film,* and *milk* is not a consequence of regional differences. These are true exceptions to the pattern.)
p, help	**25.** Next we turn our attention to the consonant *p*. In this study, we are establishing a key symbol for each phoneme in our language. The logical key symbol to use to identify the first phoneme heard in *pig* is _____ . It is the last phoneme heard in ________ . (*help, graph*)
p	**26.** We establish a key symbol and a key word to help distinguish this phoneme from any other. *Pig* is the key word we have selected to identify the sound represented by _____ .
p	**27.** Next we examine its dependability. *P*, as a single consonant, is very reliable. When we see *p,* we can expect to hear the sound we are associating with the key symbol _____ .
no *f*	**28.** Do we expect to hear the sound we associate with the key symbol *p* in *phone?* _____ . The two-letter grapheme *ph* represents the sound we associate with the key symbol _____ .
silent	**29.** Sometimes, however, the *p* has no phoneme; it is ________ . Rewrite the following words, omitting the consonant letters that represent no phonemes.
aple *hapy*	*apple* ________ *happy* ________
pupet *pupy*	*puppet* ________ *puppy* ________
no	**30.** Is *p* sounded in the following words? ________
	pseudo *psychology* *psalm* *pterodactyl* *pneumonic* *pneumonia*
	We can generalize:
p	**When *p* is followed by *s, t,* or *n* at the beginning of a word, the _____ is usually silent.**

	31. The consonants *b, h, k, l,* and *p* as single letters are very reliable.
silent	However, they are not always sounded; each has "___________ letter" patterns.

BOX 2.2

Consonant Study Guide

b, h, k, l, m, p, q, r, v

Consonant	Key Symbol	Key Word
b	*b*	*boat*
h	*h*	*hat*
k	*k*	*kite*
l	*l*	*lion*
m	*m*	*moon*
p	*p*	*pig*
q	no key symbol	no key word
r	*r*	*ring*
v	*v*	*van*

Bb is usually silent when it follows *m* or precedes *t* in the same syllable (*climb, doubt*).

Hh is silent when it follows the consonants *g* (*ghost*), *k* (*khaki*), or *r* (*rhino*). *H* is also silent when it follows a vowel (*hurrah*). Sometimes *h* is silent at the beginning of a word (*hour*).

Kk is silent at the beginning of a word or syllable when followed by *n* (*knee*).

Ll is sometimes silent when followed, in the same syllable, by *m* (*calm*), *k* (*chalk*), or *d* (*should*). If you hear an /l/ in *calm,* this is a regional difference in pronunciation.

Mm is a very dependable letter. When we see *m* in a word, we can be sure that it represents the phoneme we associate with the key word *moon.*

Pp is usually silent when followed by *s* (*psychology*), *t* (*pterodactyl*), or *n* (*pneumonia*) at the beginning of a word.

Qq has no key symbol. The *q* may represent the /*k*/ (*antique*). *Q* is almost always followed by the letter *u.* The *u* may be silent or represent the sound of the *w.* When the *u* represents the sound of *w,* the *qu* stands for *kw* (kween).

Rr is a dependable letter. When we see *r* in a word, we can be sure that it represents the sound we associate with the key word *ring.*

Vv is a dependable letter. When we see *v* in a word, we can be sure that it represents the sound we associate with the key word *van.*

Silent Consonants

Two like-consonants appearing together in a word generally represent one phoneme (*bubble, puddle, waffle, jelly, summer, dinner, puppet, carrot, buzz*).

Review 4

1. Phonics is used to decode unknown words. The pronunciation of these nonsense words is unknown to you. Using the generalizations you have studied, decide which key symbol should represent each of the underlined consonants. Rewrite the "words" omitting silent consonants.

   a. *knoh* b. *psaph* c. *mell* d. *plarrah*
   e. *ghaeve* f. *lalm* g. *khaque* h. *ptovom*
   i. *rolk* j. *rhimb* k. *quimmel* l. *kloppem*
   m. *vobter*

2. *Ph* and *ch* are examples of ____________ : each represents ____________ phoneme(s).
   (How many?)

3. Why is it difficult to pronounce /*b*/, /*k*/, and /*p*/ aloud?

4. Why did we omit *q* in our list of key symbols?

   (See the Answers section for the answers to Review 4.)

d, f, j, n, z

				1	2	3
d	*d*	*dog*	**1.** Each of the five consonants, *d, f, j, n,* and *z,* has minor irregularities. Complete the table at the right with the letter (1), key symbol (2), and key word (3) for these consonants. Select the key words from the following:	_____	_____	_____
f	*f*	*fish*		_____	_____	_____
j	*j*	*jeep*		_____	_____	_____
n	*n*	*nut*		_____	_____	_____
z	*z*	*zipper*		_____	_____	_____
			jeep *nut* *fish* *gerbil* *dog* *zipper* *moon*			

f	*f*	**2.** Say the word *fish.* Now start to say the word again but hold the first sound. This is the sound we represent by the key symbol _____ . The *f* is, in general, a reliable letter. Write the key symbol for the sound represented by *f* in each of the words at the right. Listen carefully!	*fiesta*	_____
	f		*fan*	_____
	f		*effect*	_____
	f		*off*	_____
	v		*of*	_____
	f		*if*	_____

v	**3.** The *f* represents the sound we associate with the key symbol _____ in the word *of.* (Try to pronounce *of* using /*f*/.)
silent *off*	**4.** One *f* in the word *effect* is not sounded. It is clear then that *f* can be a _____________ letter. Another example of an unsounded *f* in the list in frame 2 is in the word _____________ .
f, /*v*/ *gh* *ph*	**5.** We have noted that *f* is, in general, a reliable letter: When we see *f* in a word, we expect, when the word is spoken, to hear the sound represented by the key symbol _____ . (Exception: in *of*, the *f* = / /.) On the other hand, there are other letters which are used to stand for the sound represented by the key symbol *f.* We will digress to study them here. What letters represent the /*f*/ in the word *enough?* _____ . In the word *phonics?* _____
fone, nit, dou *enouf, gost, lam* *graf, dauter, hi*	**6.** The *gh* digraph can be silent. Rewrite these words using key symbols for all consonants and omitting silent letters. Copy the vowels as they are, pronouncing them as they would sound in the original word. *phone* ________ *knight* ________ *dough* ________ *enough* ________ *ghost* ________ *lamb* ________ *graph* ________ *daughter* ________ *high* ________
b r t *t* *s t* *t*	**7.** Study the words at the right. The *gh* digraph is usually silent when followed by _____ . What consonants are sounded in these words? *bright* _____ *sight* _____ *ought* _____
gh /*f*/ beginning *h*	**8.** Study these words: *ghost, high, rough.* The digraph _____ is silent or represents / / when it appears after the vowel in a syllable. When it appears at the __________ of the syllable, the _____ in the two-letter combination is silent.
ph	**9.** Study these words: *dolphin, graph, phrase.* The digraph _____ can be found at the beginning or end of a syllable (that is, both before and after the vowel).

foto *foneme* *fork* *alfabet* *foot* *f*	**10.** Rewrite the words at the right to indicate their pronunciation. Use the key symbols for the consonants. Copy the vowels as they appear. *photo* *phoneme* *fork* *alphabet* *foot* **The digraph *ph* represents the sound we associate with the key symbol __________ .**
first, laugh, phone *after, cough, nephew* *lift, enough, graph* *f, f, f* **silent**	**11.** We have identified three graphemes which represent /*f*/. Pronounce the words below. Underline the grapheme in each word that represents /*f*/, and write the key symbol on the line below. *first* *laugh* *phone* *after* *cough* *nephew* *lift* *enough* *graph* _____ _____ _____ **The *gh* may represent /*f*/ or it may be __________ (*high, through*).**
j *jeep*	**12.** Say *jeep* out loud. Now pronounce the first phoneme in that word. We will represent the initial sound heard in *jeep* with the key symbol _____ . *J* is a very reliable letter. When we see a *j* in a word, we will use the same sound as that in its key word __________ .
y	**13.** There is one exception! Pronounce "Hallelujah." You see a *j*, but you do not say /*j*/. Can you determine what key symbol you would use to represent the *j*? _____
juj, nowlej, ej	**14.** It might be well at this time to look at a combination of letters which represents /*j*/, the *dg.* Rewrite these words to indicate their pronunciation. (Omit each silent *e* and copy the other vowels as they are.) *judge* ________ *knowledge* ________ *edge* ________ Perhaps you hear the /*d*/, but try pronouncing the words as though /*dg*/ = /*j*/. It comes out the same, does it not?

Answers	Frames
no no *j*	**15.** Study the one-syllable words below. Does the *dg* digraph occur at the beginning of English words? _____ (yes, no) At the end of English words? _____ (yes, no) *fudge* *budget* *dodge* *pidgin* *judge* *gadget* **The *dg* is a very reliable digraph. What key symbol do we use to represent the phoneme?** __________
d	**16.** We shall represent the initial phoneme heard in *dog* with the key symbol _____ . Say *dog* aloud. Listen carefully as you say the initial phoneme in *dog.*
lader, suden	**17.** The *d* is fairly dependable. It, however, may be silent as in *ladder* and *sudden.* Rewrite these words omitting silent consonants. *ladder* __________ *sudden* __________
t	**18.** But let us examine more closely the sounds the *d* represents. The key symbol represents the sounds heard in *doll, did, day, led.* Now read these words out loud to discover another sound that the *d* represents: *jumped, clipped, hoped, missed.* These *d*s represent the sound we associate with the key symbol _____ .
hopt *jumpt* *slipt* one	**19.** Study each word at the right. *Missed,* for example, has four phonemes. Rewrite each word showing the pronunciation of the consonants by using key symbols. *missed* *mist* *hoped* __________ *jumped* __________ *slipped* __________ In spite of their appearance, these are all __________-syllable words. (one, two)

t one *d*	**20.** We have noted that the *d* sometimes is pronounced as though it were _____ (as in *kissed*). Now examine the words below. They are also ____________-syllable words. The final consonant represents the sound we associate with the key symbol _____ . *played* *smiled* *called*
two *ed* *d* *t, d*	**21.** Notice the sound the *d* represents when *ed* forms a separate syllable. Say each of these words out loud. These are ____________-syllable words. In each the suffix _____ forms a separate syllable. The final *d* represents the sound assigned to the key symbol _____ . Look at the letters preceding the suffixes (*seated*). They are either _____ or _____ . *seated* *wanted* *waited* *needed* *sanded* *folded*
syllable, *d* *d*	**22.** **In general, the suffix *ed* forms a separate ____________ when it is preceded by *t* or _____ .** When the *ed* forms a separate syllable, the final *d* represents the sound we associate with the key symbol _____ .
d ***t***	**23.** To summarize: **When the suffix *ed* forms a separate syllable, the *d* represents the sound associated with the key symbol _____ . When the suffix does not form a separate syllable, the *d* may represent the sound associated with the key symbol *d* or with the key symbol _____ .**
/j/ soljer fuj	**24.** We have noted that *dg* forms a special combination representing / /. Occasionally a *d* or *di* represents the */j/*. Perhaps you hear */j/* when you pronounce *graduation.* Rewrite these words using key symbols to represent the consonant sounds and omitting any silent letters. *soldier* ____________ *fudge* ____________

sudden *jumped* *soldier* *fudge*	**25.** We have seen that *d* can be silent as in ______________ (*sudden, debt*). *D* can represent /*t*/ as in ______________ (*jumped, pulled*), and /*j*/ as in ______________ (*gem, soldier*), and /*j*/ as a part of the combination *dg* as in ______________ (*fudge, handgrip*).
nut *colum* *maner*	**26.** The /*n*/, identified by the first phoneme in the key word ______________, can be silent as in *running* and when preceded by *m* as in *hymn.* Rewrite these words omitting silent letters. *column* ______________ *manner* ______________
1 yes, 2 no	**27.** *N* is very reliable, with one common but confusing exception. First, let us note that *n* is a part of the digraph *ng* as heard in *sing.* The *n* and the *g* represent _____ (How many?) phoneme(s) in *sing.* Is *ng* a digraph in *bring?* ______________ (yes or no) The *n* and *g* represent _____ (How many?) phoneme(s) in *ungrateful.* Is the *ng* a digraph in *ungrateful?* ______________ (yes or no)
yes *think*	**28.** Say *thing.* Is the *ng* a digraph? ______________ . Add the phoneme represented by *k* to *thing* (*thing* + *k*). We do not spell this word *thingk:* We spell it ______________ . The letter *n* represents /*ng*/ in *think!*
thang + *k*	**29.** There are many words in which you hear /*ng*/ but see only *n.* These words follow a pattern: Generally the letter following the *n* is either *k* or *g.* Pronounce *thank.* Which of these "keys to pronunciation" is correct? ______________ *than* + *k* *thang* + *k*

fing ger	**30.** Pronounce the "words" at the right. This is hard! Which set of key symbols (consonant sounds only) indicates the correct pronunciation of *finger?* ____________ *fin ger* *fing ger* *fing er*
ng *g*	**31.** In *finger,* the *n* represents the sound we associate with the key symbol _____ . The *g* represents the sound we associate with the key symbol _____ . To show pronunciation, we need both the *ng* and the *g.*
kang ga roo *sing gle*	**32.** Which set of symbols below indicates the pronunciation of *kangaroo?* Of *single?* *kan ga roo* *kang ga roo* ____________ *sin gle* *sing le* *sing gle* ____________
ran *bank (bangk)*	**33.** It is clear that the grapheme *n* sometimes represents the phoneme associated with the key symbol *n,* as in ____________ , (*ran, rang*) and sometimes with the digraph *ng,* as in ____________ . (*bank, band*)
engage	**34.** We have also noted that when we see *n* and *g* together in a word, the *ng* may represent the two separate phonemes that we associate with the separate symbols *n* and *g* as in ____________ . (*engage, clang*)
solemn *banker*	**35.** We have seen that the letter *n* may be silent as in ____________ . (*solemn, rang*) The single letter *n* may also represent the /*ng*/ as in ____________ . (*ingredient, banker*)
zipper *buzz*	**36.** The key symbol *z* represents the phoneme heard at the beginning of its key word ____________ . In general, it is fairly reliable. It may be silent as, for example, one *z* is silent in ____________ . (*zigzag, buzz*)

Before beginning to work through the phonics program, be certain to read the introduction section in the text. Then cut the mask from the cover along the line of the fold.

Place the mask on the answer column, study the text, write your response, and move the mask down to check your answer. Please be certain to write your answer ***first***, as answering the questions mentally or glancing at the answers first will defeat the purpose of the program.

To avoid the distraction of the type and color used on this side of the mask, you may find it helpful to use the mask with the reverse, blank side up. You may also find the mask useful as a bookmark.

Why Z Comes Last

ays been the last letter of the alphabet. Thousands of years ago, *Z* was the
oenician (tenth-century B.C.) and the Greek (eighth-century B.C.)
reeks passed their alphabet to the ancient Romans, the letter *Z* became
et as well. Although the *Z* represented a speech sound in the Greek
real purpose in Latin because the Latin language did not use the sound
er. The *Z* may have stayed in the Latin alphabet had it not been for the fact
nted two Latin phonemes, the /k/ in *kite* and the voiced /g/ in *goat*. The
the voiced /g/ its own letter, so they introduced a new letter, the letter *G*.
visually quite similar, which is not surprising since the Romans created the
e letter *C*. To keep the order of the letters in the Latin alphabet intact, the
ete the useless letter *Z*, and to replace it with the newly created letter *G*.
e the seventh letter in the Latin alphabet, as it is in our own English
ntact with the Greeks made it necessary for the Romans to translate Greek
mans found that they needed to add the letter *Z* to the Latin alphabet.
its old slot as the seventh letter would have changed the letter sequence,
did not want to do. The Romans solved their problem by adding the letter
abet, where it remains today in our own English alphabet.

teries of the alphabet: The origins of writing. (J. Bacon, Trans.) New York, NY: Abbeville

37. The *z* occasionally stands for the sound represented by the key symbol _____ as in *quartz* and the *zh* as in ______________ .
(*seize, azure*)

Pronounce *seize* and *azure* aloud. Which has the phoneme you hear in *zoo?* ______________

38. Check the words at the right in which the *z* stands for the phoneme heard at the beginning of the word *zipper.*

zero
waltz
prize
azure

BOX 2.4

Consonant and Digraph Study Guide

d, f, j, n, z

Digraphs *dg, gh, ph*

-ed Suffix

Consonant	Key Symbol	Key Word
d	*d*	*dog*
f	*f*	*fish*
j	*j*	*jeep*
n	*n*	*nut*
z	*z*	*zipper*

Digraph	Key Symbol	Key Word
dg	*j*	*jeep*
gh	*f, g,* or silent	*fish, goat,* or no key word when silent
ph	*f*	*fish*

Suffix	Key Symbol	Key Word
-ed	*d*	*dog* (fold*ed*)
-ed	*t*	*table* (hop*ed*)

Dd may be silent (*ladder*), or may represent /t/ (*jumped*) when part of the *-ed* suffix.

Ff is, in general, a reliable letter, with a notable exception in the word *of,* in which the letter *f* represents /v/.

Jj is a very reliable letter (*jelly*).

Nn may be silent when preceded by *m* (*autumn*). The single *n* may represent /ng/ (*thank*).

Zz represents the /z/ in the key word *zipper,* and occasionally stands for /s/ (*waltz*) and the /zh/ in *azure.*

gh The *gh* digraph is usually silent when followed by *t* in a syllable (*night*). The *gh* is silent (*through*), or represents /f/ (*cough*) when it appears after the vowel in a syllable. When *gh* occurs at the beginning of a word, the *h* is silent (*ghost*). There are only a handful of English words that begin with *gh.* They include: *ghost, ghetto, ghastly,* and *ghoul.*

dg The *dg* digraph represents /j/ (*fudge, budget*).

ph The *ph* digraph represents /f/, and may occur at the beginning (*phone*), or end (*graph*) of a syllable (that is, before or after the vowel).

-ed Suffix The *-ed* suffix forms a separate syllable when it is preceded by *t* or *d* (*salted, folded*). When the *-ed* forms a separate syllable, the final *d* represents /d/ (*folded*). When the suffix does not form a separate syllable, the *d* may represent the sound associated with /d/ (*played*), or with /t/ (*hoped*).

	39. We have noted that the consonants *d, f, j, n,* and *z* have irregularities. In the next two frames, select the word at the right which illustrates the irregularity described.
	The consonant may represent a phoneme other than that of its key symbol:
of	*f* = /*v*/ *fish, of*
missed	*d* = /*t*/ *missed, list*
bank	*n* = /*ng*/ *bank, bone*
waltz	*z* = /*s*/ *zoo, waltz*
azure	*z* = /*zh*/ *his, azure*
	40. **The key symbol may be represented by a different letter or digraph:**
phone	*ph* = /*f*/ *phone, puff*
rough	*gh* = /*f*/ *bough, rough*
fudge	*dg* = /*j*/ *jug, fudge*

Review 5

1. Write the key symbols that represent the sounds of the consonant letters in these words:

a. *bough*	**b.** *tough*	**c.** *hedge*	**d.** *of*	**e.** *phone*
f. *tight*	**g.** *ghastly*	**h.** *soldier*	**i.** *gender*	**j.** *huffed*
k. *planted*	**l.** *quilt*	**m.** zero	**n.** *sleigh*	**o.** *column*

2. In which words do you hear the same phoneme as that represented by the underlined part of the first word?

   a. *dog*   *clapped*   *don't*   *ride*   *soldier*   *moved*
   b. *fish*   *fine*   *graph*   *of*   *photo*   *off*
   c. *jeep*   *wedge*   *soldier*   *gold*   *hallelujah*   *Roger*
   d. *nut*   *sling*   *hymn*   *knot*   *stranger*   *lank*
   e. *zipper*   *his*   *puzzle*   *does*   *seizure*   *waltz*

   (See the Answers section for the answers to Review 5.)

c, g, w, y

g *g* *goat* *w* *w* *wagon* *y* *y* *yo-yo*	**1.** Each of the four consonants *c, g, w,* and *y* is very irregular. However, each has a pattern of consistency within its inconsistencies. The *c* and *g* have some patterns in common as do the *w* and *y. C* has been omitted in the table at the right because it has no phoneme of its own. Complete the table for each of the other three with the key symbol (2) and key word (3). Select the words from the following: *yo-yo, jeep, wagon, why, goat, kite, van, city* 1 2 3 *g* ______ ______ *w* ______ ______ *y* ______ ______
goat *guess* *glass* *go* *begin*	**2.** *G* is the key symbol for the phoneme we hear at the beginning of its key word ______________ . Check its reliability: Does it always represent the sound we associate with the *g* in *goat?* Pronounce these words using /*g*/ whenever you see a *g*. Then pronounce them correctly. Check those in which you hear /*g*/. *guess* *huge* *page* *ginger* *glass* *go* *enough* *gnat* *begin* *sing*
guess, glass, go *begin* *huge* *page, ginger* *gnat* *enough, sing*	**3.** It is clear that *g* is a very unreliable letter. In the words above, *g* represents its hard sound (/*g*/ as in *goat*) in the words ______________ , ______________ , ______________ , and ______________ . *G* represents the soft phoneme, /*j*/, in the words ______________ , ______________ and ______________ . *G* is silent when followed by *n* as in ______________ . *G* is part of a digraph, representing a different sound from either of its components in ______________ and ______________ .

 j *j* *g*	**4.** *G* is the key symbol for the hard sound we hear at the beginning of *goat.* We have noted that the letter *g* often represents the soft sound we associate with the key symbol _____ . Are these used interchangeably or is there a pattern to the words which might give a clue as to whether the *g* represents the soft sound we associate with the key symbol _____ or the hard sound we identify with the key symbol _____ ? Let us examine some known words to see.
1. *gate* 2. *gem* 3. *giant* 4. *gone* 5. *gum* 6. *gym*	**5.** Study the sets of words below. Add a word from the list at the right to each set. Choose a word in which the *g* represents the same phoneme as the other underlined letters in the set and has the same vowel following the underlined *g*. *gone* *gem* *gum* *get* *gym* *gate* *giant*

1	2	3	4	5	6
gain	*gentle*	*giraffe*	*go*	*gulp*	*gypsy*
against	*age*	*engine*	*wagon*	*regular*	*energy*
________	________	________	________	________	________

e, i, y	**6. The letter *g* usually represents the sound we associate with the key symbol *j* (the soft sound) when it is followed by the vowels _____ , _____ , or _____ .** Carefully study the sets of words above before you answer.
get *j, get*	**7.** The word *usually* in the generalization indicates that this is not always true. The word ____________ (*gem, get*) is an exception. When *g* is followed by the letter *e,* the *g* usually represents the sound we associate with the key symbol _____ . The word ____________ (*get, gentle*) does not follow this generalization.

a, o, u	**8.** Make a generalization about the phoneme that we associate with the key symbol *g:* **The letter *g* usually represents the sound we associate with the key symbol *g* when it is followed by the vowels _____ , _____ , or _____ .**
e, i, y hard (or the one associated with g)	**9.** What happens when other letters follow *g?* Study the words at the right. The generalization will read: The *g* usually represents the soft sound when followed by _____ , _____ , or _____ . When followed by any other letter or when it appears at the end of a word, the *g* represents the ____________ sound. *great* *ghost* *pilgrim* *gleam* *egg* Memorize these sets: /*j*/—*e i y* /*g*/—*a o u* You may wish to compose a phrase to help you remember, as "*an ornery ugly goat.*"
e, i, y *g*	**10.** Do not forget that there are exceptions. The generalization above, however, is a useful one. When you see a word you do not recognize, a word which contains a *g,* try the generalization. Try the phoneme represented by the key symbol *j* when the *g* is followed by _____ , _____ , or _____ ; otherwise, try the hard sound, represented by the key symbol _____ .
j yes	**11.** Many words end in the letters *ge.* Pronounce the words at the right. The key symbol that represents the final sound in each of these words is ______________ . Does the generalization apply to words that end in the letters *ge?* ______________ *huge* *sponge* *cage* *orange*

guard, guilt, ej
gastly, naw, paj
guilt

12. Rewrite these words to show the pronunciation of the consonant letters. Omit each silent consonant and the silent ***e*** s. Copy the other vowels as they are.

guard ____________ *guilt* ____________ *edge* ____________

ghastly ____________ *gnaw* ____________ *page* ____________

(It is interesting to note that an unnecessary *u* has been added to many words which "makes the *g* hard" and so eliminates many exceptions, for example, ____________ above.)

---

symbol
word

13. The letter *c* is also very irregular, but on top of that, it has no phoneme of its own, and therefore, no key ____________ or key ____________ . (See Frame 1, page 29.)

---

c
k
s

14. Study these words: *cute, city.* Both start with the letter _____ . The first phoneme in *cute* represents the sound we associate with the key symbol _____ . The first phoneme in *city* represents the sound we associate with the key symbol _____ .

---

k *s*

15. As a single letter grapheme, the *c* not only represents no phoneme of its own, but commonly serves to represent two other phonemes, the _____ and the _____ .

There are some clues to guide us to the sounds the *c* represents in words we do not know.

---

1. *cat* 2. *cent* 3. *city*
4. *coat* 5. *curl*
6. *bicycle*

16. Study the sets of words below.

For each set, choose a word from the six at the right in which the *c* represents the same phoneme as the other underlined letters in the set and has the same vowel following it.

coat
bicycle
city
curl
cent
cat

1	2	3	4	5	6
cane	*center*	*circus*	*cook*	*current*	*cymbal*
became	*mice*	*decide*	*bacon*	*circus*	*encyclopedia*
________	________	________	________	________	________

Check to see if you followed the directions.

BOX 2.5

Why Not *K* for *Cat*?

Alphabetically speaking, the letter C has a rather checkered past. The Greeks called the letter C, *gamma,* and used it to represent the voiced /g/ heard in *goat* (the hard *g*). The Etruscans, who inherited the alphabet from the Greeks, did not use the voiced /g/ in their spoken language. Rather than eliminate the letter C altogether, the Etruscans decided to use it to represent the /k/ heard in *kite.* In changing the sound represented by the gamma from a /g/ to a /k/, the Etruscan alphabet came to represent /k/ with four different letter sequences. In the Etruscan alphabet, the /k/ could be represented with *ka, ce* or *ci,* and *qu!* The Etruscan alphabet subsequently passed to the Latin alphabet, and eventually to our own English alphabet. Today we continue the practice that was passed down from the Etruscans, using the same three letters to represent the /k/ in English words: *k, c,* and *q* (as in *antique*).

Ouaknin, M.C. (1999). *Mysteries of the alphabet: The origins of writing.* (J. Bacon, Trans.) New York, NY: Abbeville Press Publishers.

1, 4, 5 *a, o, u*	**17.** Which sets of words in frame 16 have **c** s that represent the hard sound, that of the /*k*/? ____________ What vowels follow the *c* in each of these groups? ____________
a, o, u	**18.** Complete the generalization: **The letter *c* usually represents the sound we associate with the *k* when it is followed by _____, _____, or _____.**
s, e, i, y	**19.** What about the soft sound? **The letter *c* usually represents the sound we associate with the _____ when it is followed by _____, _____, or _____.**
The letter *g* usually represents the soft sound *(j)* when it is followed by *e, i,* or *y.*	**20.** What is the generalization about the phoneme we associate with the soft sound of *g?*

yes a, o, u e, i, y a o u	**21.** Are there similarities between the generalizations concerning the sounds represented by *c* and *g?* ______________ The combined generalization might read: The consonants *c* and *g* represent their hard sounds when followed by _____ , _____ , and _____ . They usually represent their soft sounds when followed by _____ , _____ , and _____ . If you remembered the phrase "*an ornery ugly goat*," you might relate it to "*an ornery ugly kid*." *C* generally represents the sound heard in *kid* when followed by _____ , _____ , or _____ .
k g hard hard	**22.** Study the words at the right. What happens when other letters follow *c* and *g?* The *c* then represents the sound we associate with _____ and the *g* the sound we associate with _____ . These are the ______________ sounds. What happens when *c* or *g* is the last letter in the word? In that position they also represent their ______________ sounds. *regret* *glad* *crow* *comic* *climb* *big*
hard	**23.** Let us summarize the generalizations: **The *c* and *g* usually represent their soft sounds when followed by *e, i,* or *y.* When followed by any other letter or when they appear at the end of the word, the *c* and the *g* represent their ______________ sounds.**
cello *girl* *gift* *give*	**24.** Now apply the generalizations to the words at the right. Place a check mark next to the words that do not follow the generalization. *cube* *giant* *cello* *girl* *cotton* *guide* *cash* *gift* *receive* *give*

silent *siense* *skool* *sene* *skalp* *skale* *skold* *skreen* *skum*	**25.** There are many words in which *s* is followed by *c*. Examine the first word at the right. Note that *c* can be a _____ letter. Rewrite each word using key symbols for the consonants. *science* _______ *school* _______ *scene* _______ *scalp* _______ *scale* _______ *scold* _______ *screen* _______ *scum* _______
ch *k*	**26.** You have learned that *c*, as a single letter, is unnecessary. Examine these words: *chair, child, check.* We have no substitute for the *c* in the digraph _____ . We cannot get along without the *c*. We could get along without the *q*, because _____ substitutes perfectly.
only one is sounded	**27.** Complete the generalization: **When two like-consonants appear together in a word, usually** _______________ .
k *s*	**28.** Does this hold for the *c?* This generalization does not hold when the consonants represent different sounds. In the word *success,* the first *c* represents the sound we associate with the key symbol _____ , the second *c* the sound we associate with the key symbol _____ .
akses, stoping *skil, aksident* *aksept, aksent*	**29.** Examine the following words. Rewrite them using key symbols for the consonants. Omit the silent letters. *access* _______ *stopping* _______ *skill* _______ *accident* _______ *accept* _______ *accent* _______

c *n, k* *blok* *duk* *blak* *bak*	**30.** In words containing *ck,* the _____ is usually silent. What consonants are sounded in *knock?* _____ . Rewrite the words at the right to show pronunciation of the consonants. *block* _______ *duck* _______ *black* _______ *back* _______
a, o, u, end letter (consonant) digraph, *ch,* silent	**31.** *C* and *g* generally represent their hard sound when followed by _____ , _____ , _____ , or come at the _____________ of a word, or are followed by another _____________ . Both *c* and *g* are part of a _____________ (*c* in _____ , *g* in *gh*). Both *c* and *g* can be _____________ as in *back* and *gnome.*
y	**32.** Say *yo-yo* aloud. Listen to the first phoneme as you pronounce this key word again. The initial sound heard in *yo-yo* will be identified by the key symbol _____ .
yo-yo *yellow young canyon* consonant	**33.** The *y* is very unreliable. You cannot assume that, when you see *y* in a word, it will represent the sound you hear in its key word ______ . Pronounce these words aloud, use /*y*/ for each *y* you see: *yellow sky rhyme young sadly play canyon* Underline those in which the *y* represents the phoneme you hear in *yo-yo.* When *y* represents the phoneme heard in *yo-yo,* it is a _____________ .
beginning	**34.** Now pronounce the above words correctly. Listen to the sound represented by the *y* in each word. You will notice when the *y* is at the _____________ of a word or a syllable it has the /*y*/ phoneme. (beginning, end)
vowel	**35.** You will notice also that each *y* within or at the end of a syllable has a _____________ sound. (consonant, vowel)

consonant */y/*	**36.** The *y* is unreliable, but there is a distinct pattern to help us select those which are consonants. When the *y* appears at the beginning of a syllable, it is a ____________ and has the sound we associate with _____ . (Exception: some words in chemistry with a foreign origin, as (another vowel, /y/) in *Ytterbia.*)
consonant *yo-yo*	**37.** As a consonant, *y* is very reliable. When we see a *y* at the beginning of a syllable, we can be sure it is a ____________ and represents the sound heard in its key word ____________ .
w *consonant*	**38.** Say *wagon* aloud. Listen to the first phoneme as you pronounce this key word again. The initial sound heard will be identified by the key symbol _____ . The *w* is very unreliable. Like the *y,* it serves as a vowel as well as a ____________ .
went *always*	**39.** Use the words at the right for this and the following five frames (40–44) to illustrate the characteristics of the consonant *w. W,* as a consonant, always appears before the vowel in a syllable. (Note: *w* as a vowel always follows another vowel.) *W* is generally an initial consonant in a word or syllable as in ____________ and in (select a two-syllable word) ____________ . *once*, *quilt*, *went*, *write*, *antique*, *who*, *snow*, *dwell*, *one*, *queen*, *always*
dwell (quilt and *queen* are okay, too!*)*	**40.** The phoneme represented by *w* may, however, be part of a blend of two consonants as in ____________ .
quilt *queen*	**41.** The grapheme *u,* when following *q,* often represents the consonant phoneme we associate with the key symbol *w.* We hear this when we say the words ____________ and ____________ .

write	**42.** The *w* is silent before *r* as in ______________ .
who (hoo)	**43.** Occasionally the letter *w* fools us. It appears to be a part of the digraph *wh* but is actually silent, as in ______________ . (This is a puzzle. Can you solve it?) Remember to refer to frame 39.
one *once*	**44.** We are familiar with the word *won.* But note the grapheme we use in the word pronounced the same but spelled ______________ . We use the same grapheme to represent the *w* in ______________ .
vowel before *away, wring*	**45.** The *w* may be a consonant or a ______________ . As a consonant, it appears ______________ (before, after) the vowel in the syllable and represents the phoneme heard in __________ (away, blow). It is sometimes silent as in _________ (wish, wring).
unreliable */g/, /j/* */ng/* */f/, silent*	**46.** We have been studying four _________ (reliable, unreliable) consonants: *c, g, w, y.* We have found that *g* may have the sound of / /, as in *goat;* or / / as in *genius;* it may be a part of a digraph which has the sound of / / as in *sing* or / / as in *enough.* It may be ______________ as in *gnaw.*
It has no key symbol of its own.	**47.** What is the distinctive key symbol for *c?*
/k/, /s/ *h,* digraph */ch/,* silent	**48.** *C* may represent the sound of / / as in *acorn* or of / / as in *nice.* It may, with the letter _____ , form a ______________ as in *much,* having the sound of / /. It is ______________ in *scissors.*
e, i *y, /k/, a* *o, u,* consonant end of a word, */j/* *e, i, y; /g/* *a, o, u,* consonant end of a word	**49.** *C* usually has its soft sound when followed by _____ , _____ , _____ . It usually has its hard sound, / /, when followed by _____ , _____ , _____ , any other ______________ , or comes at the ______________ . *G* usually represents its soft sound / / when followed by _____ , _____ , _____ ; and its hard sound / / when followed by _____ , _____ , _____ , any other ______________ , or comes at the ______________ .

	50. **The consonants *w* and *y* are positioned before the vowel in a syllable. The consonant *y* is never silent. The consonant *w* may be silent**
wrote, two, who	as in the words (check those correct) *quit, wrote, wing, two, who. W*
digraph	may be a part of a ____________ as in *white.*

Review 6

1. What generalization helps you to determine the sound of /*g*/ in an unknown word?
2. Write the key symbols for the consonants in these words:

   a. *giant* b. *bank* c. *girl* d. *big* e. *machine*
   f. *cook* g. *who* h. *match* i. *yellow* j. *way*
   k. *quick* l. *write* m. *yet* n. *knack*

3. Which of the above contains an exception to the "hard-soft *g*" generalization?
4. What generalization helps you to determine the sound of a *c* in an unknown word?
5. The suffix *-ed* may have the sound of / / as in *quilted,* of / / as in *called,* of / / as in *jumped.*
6. What generalization helps you to determine whether *w* represents /*w*/ and *y* represents /*y*/?
7. What key symbol indicates the pronunciation of the last phoneme in each of the following words.

   a. *beg* b. *church* c. *judge* d. *quack* e. *knowledge*
   f. *back* g. *ache* h. *unique* i. *critic* j. *rough*

8. The two-letter key symbols *ch* and *ng* are called ____________ .
9. Rewrite the following words using key symbols to indicate the pronunciation of the underlined parts. Omit silent consonant letters. Underline the digraphs.

   range ____________ *wrinkle* ____________ *ransom* ____________
   manger ____________ *triangle* ____________ *links* ____________

10. As a single letter, we can expect *g* to represent the hard sound we associate with the key symbol *g,* except when followed by _____ , _____ , or _____ .

11. When *g* is part of a __________ as in *enough,* it is not considered a single letter consonant: The *g* in *enough* does <u>not</u> represent the sound we associate with the key symbol *g* as in __________ .
(*go, ginger*)

The *g* in *enough* does <u>not</u> represent the sound we associate with the key symbol _____ as in *gem.*

Nor is the *g* in *enough* a __________ letter as it is in *knight.*

(See the Answers section for the answers to Review 6.)

s, t, x

s *s* *sun* *t* *t* *table*	**1.** The three consonants *s, t,* and *x* are unreliable. You cannot assume that when you see one of them in a word, you will hear the same phoneme as that in its key word. Complete the table adding key symbols (2) and key words (3). Select key words from this set: *city, sun, chin, she, table, zipper, ax, thin.* 1 2 3 *s* _____ _________ *t* _____ _________
boks	**2.** Why is there no *x* in the table above? The letter *x* has no key symbol because it has no distinctive sound of its own. It represents sounds we associate with other key symbols. Pronounce *box* aloud. Try to write *box* using other letters: _____________ .
egzact (or *egzakt*) *box* *gz* Either is correct.	**3.** Pronounce *exact.* Rewrite it using other key symbols: _____________ . The letter *x* represents the sounds we associate with *ks* in _____________ and _____ as in *exact.* And we often interchange (*box, exam*) them! How do you pronounce *exit?* _____________ . (*egzit, eksit*) We are more apt to use /*gz*/ when *x* appears between two vowel phonemes.
/*ks*/, /*gz*/	**4.** We have seen that *x* may represent the phonemes / / or / /. This may sound confusing, but it presents no problem to an English-speaking person, who will automatically use the acceptable phoneme.

  z *eks*	**5.** Then consider the word *xylophone.* At the beginning of a word, *x* consistently represents the sound we associate with the key symbol _____ . Of course, at times we use *x* as a letter; such as *X-ray.* In this instance, _____ could be used as the grapheme to represent the *x.*
siks *zylofone* *egzample* *boks* *zeroks* *egzist*	**6. The *x* could be omitted from our alphabet by using the letters *gz, ks,* or *z.*** Spell the words at the right, substituting the proper graphemes for the letter *x* in each one. *six* ______________ *xylophone* ______________ *example* ______________ *box* ______________ *Xerox* ______________ *exist* ______________
 k *gz, ks, z* *ch* *s, k*	**7.** The phonemes represented by *c, q,* and *x* need no key symbols. In our one-to-one correspondence they are already represented. We could omit the letter *q* entirely by substituting the _____ . We could omit the letter *x* by substituting _____ , _____ , or _____ . We do use the *c* as part of the digraph _____ , but as a single letter, the _____ (*city*) and _____ (*coat*) could adequately take its place.
s *sun* yes, no, no no, no is not cannot	**8.** The phoneme represented by *s* (key symbol _____) is heard in its key word ______________ . Does it represent the sound heard in *list?* ______________ *has?* ______________ *she?* ______________ *was?* ______________ *surely?* ______________ The letter *s* ______________ (is, is not) very reliable. When you see the letter *s* in a word you ______________ (can, cannot) be sure you will hear /*s*/ when it is pronounced.
s *s* *z*	**9.** Say the words at the right aloud. Listen very carefully to the underlined part. Which key symbol represents each part? Write it in the space following the word. *this* _____ *history* _____ *his* _____

	10. The grapheme *s* is used to represent different phonemes. Study the words at the right. The single consonant *s* represents the sound we usually associate	*see* *ask*
see, ask	with *s* in the words __________ and __________	*rose*
rose, his	with *z* in the words __________ and __________	*his*
sure, sugar	with *sh* in the words __________ and __________	*sure*
television, treasure	with *zh* in the words __________ and __________	*sugar* *television* *treasure*
z *z*	**11.** Pronounce *his* and *has* aloud. The key symbol that represents the final sound in these words is _____. There are many words in which the grapheme *s* represents the / /. Write the key symbol for each of the plural endings of the words below. If you have trouble, try both the /*s*/ and the /*z*/. You must say them aloud.	
	toys *dogs* *beds* *cats* *hops*	
z, z, z, s, s	____ ____ ____ ____ ____	
sizorz *zylofon* *fuzy* *us* *uz* *fuz* *miks*	**12.** Rewrite the words at the right using the key symbol that represents the sound of each consonant. Copy the vowels as they are but omit the silent *e*s.	*scissors* ________ *xylophone* ________ *fuzzy* ________ *us* ________ *use* ________ *fuse* ________ *mix* ________

	13. The consonant *s* is unreliable: It often represents the phonemes we associate with *z, sh,* and *zh,* as well as its key symbol *s.* Rewrite the following words using *s, z, sh,* or *zh* to indicate the sound the *s* represents. Copy the vowels as they are, pronouncing them as they sound in the real word.
rugz, iz, doez	*rugs* ____________ *is* ____________ *does* ____________
peaz, some, pleazhure	*peas* ____________ *some* ____________ *pleasure* ____________
whoze, so, shurely	*whose* ____________ *so* ____________ *surely* ____________
	14. When we see an *s* in an unknown word, we have few clues to tell us which phoneme it represents. We might note the following: (1) The letter *s* usually represents the sound we associate with the
s, sun	key symbol _____ . It is the sound heard in ______________ . (*sun, sure*)
	(2) Except for certain foreign names (as *Saar*), the *s* at the beginning
miss	of a word stands for the sound heard in ______________ . (*miss, whose*) (3) Except when acting as a plural, the *s* at the end of words represents /*s*/ or /*z*/ with about equal frequency. (4) We tend to use the phoneme represented by the *z,* the voiced counterpart of /*s*/, when the preceding phoneme is voiced. (English-speaking people use the correct ending automatically, thus we have not studied voice-voiceless phonemes in this edition.)
	15. The letter *t* as a single consonant (as heard in its key word
table	______________) is fairly reliable. However, we must distinguish between *t* as a single letter and *t* as part of a digraph. Pronounce these words: *this, think, with.* We do not hear /*t*/ in the two-letter
th	grapheme _____ . We will study this grapheme later.
	16. But then pronounce these words: *Thomas, thyme.* (Exceptions! Exceptions!) The *th* in each of these words does represent the
/*t*/, *h*	phoneme / /. Or we could say that the _____ is silent.

no, *shun*	**17.** One of the common "endings" in our language is found in these words: *motion, convention, station.* Pronounce them. Do you hear /*t*/? ____________ This ending could be spelled ____________ . (*shun, ton*)
/*ch*/ /*ch*/ /*t*/ /*ch*/ /*sh*/	**18.** Examine these words. Pronounce them, paying special attention to the underlined parts. What phoneme does each part represent? Work carefully. *righteous* / / *question* / / *mountain* / / *natural* / / *action* / /
beginning	**19.** It is clear there are many word "parts" (never at the ____________ of the word) in which the *t*, in combination with a (beginning, ending) vowel, represents a phoneme other than /*t*/.
silent	**20.** Pronounce these words: *bouquet, beret, debut.* There are several common words derived from the French language in which the *t* is ____________ .
t *often* *soften* *listen* *fasten* *moisten*	**21.** When *t* follows *f* or *s*, the _____ is sometimes silent. These words are written without the silent consonants; write them correctly: *ofen* ____________ *sofen* ____________ *lisen* ____________ *fasen* ____________ *moisen* ____________
match, watch, hatch	**22.** The *t* is also silent in the *tch* combinations. Pronounce the words below saying the /*ch*/ as in *chair.* Spell them correctly. *mach* ____________ *wach* ____________ *hach* ____________

	23. The *t* is fairly reliable. However, it may be silent and often loses the /*t*/ phoneme when combined with other letters.	
	The words at the right will aid you in filling in the blanks below. We have noted that *t*, as a single letter, is fairly reliable.	*catch* *father*
soften	It may be silent as when it follows *f* (as in ______________)	*soften*
s listen, ch	or _____ (as in ______________) and when it precedes _____	*letter*
catch	(as in ______________). Only one *t* is sounded in such words	*listen*
letter	as ______________ . It may also be silent in words adopted	*future*
ballet	from the French as ______________ . In connection with a	*lotion*
future	vowel, the *t* may represent /*ch*/ as in ______________ or	*ballet*
lotion	/*sh*/ as in ______________ . It is often a part of a consonant	
father	digraph as in ______________ , in which case the /*t*/ is not heard.	

ng z t	**24.** We have noted that several different graphemes may represent the initial sound heard in *sun* as well as the initial sound heard in *zipper.* To illustrate, write the key symbol that indicates the pronunciation of each of the consonants in the words at the right.	*anxiety*	______________
z		*is*	______________
t s		*its*	______________
s n t		*scent*	______________
z n z		*zones*	______________
s r k l	(If you get these, you are really thinking!)	*circle*	______________
z l f n		*xylophone*	______________

sugar	**25.** We have also noted that the grapheme *s* may represent sounds other than that heard in *sun,* and that the grapheme *z* occasionally represents sounds other than that heard in *zipper.* Check the words at the right in which the *s* stands for a phoneme other than that heard at the beginning of *sun.*	*sugar*	______________
		this	______________
pleasure		*pleasure*	______________
		whisp	______________
hose		*hose*	______________

ks, gz, z	**26.** We called *x* an unnecessary letter because it could be replaced by _____ in *ax,* by _____ in *example,* and by _____ in *xylophone.*

BOX 2.6

Consonant Study Guide

c, g, s, t, w, x, y

Consonant	Key Symbol	Key Word
c	*no key symbol*	*no key word*
g	*g*	*goat*
s	*s*	*sun*
t	*t*	*table*
w	*w*	*wagon*
x	no key symbol	no key word
y	*y*	*yo-yo*

Cc does not have a key symbol. *C* usually represents /s/ (the soft sound) when it is followed by *e* (*see*), *i* (*side*), or *y* (*system*). *C* usually represents /k/ (the hard sound) when followed by *a* (*cat*), *o* (*coat*), or *u* (*cut*), when it appears at the end of a word (*comic*), and when followed by any other letter (*cloud*).

Gg may represent /j/ (the soft sound) when it is followed by the vowels *e* (*gerbil*), *i* (*giant*), or *y* (*gypsy*), although with exceptions. *G* usually represents /g/ (the hard sound) when it is followed by *a* (*gate*), *o* (*go*), or *u* (*gum*), when it appears at the end of a word (*leg*), and when followed by any other letter (*glass*).

Ss, except when acting as a plural at the end of words, represents /s/ (*miss*) or /z/ (*whose*) with about equal frequency. *S* also represents /zh/ (*television*), and occasionally stands for */sh/* (*sugar*).

Tt may be silent when it follows the letter s (*listen*) or *f* (*soften*), and when it precedes *ch* (*catch*). In connection with a vowel, *t* may represent /ch/ (*future*) or /sh/ (*station*). When part of a digraph (*th*), the *t* is not heard (*father*). *T* may also be silent in words adopted from the French language (*ballet*).

Ww serves as a consonant and a vowel. As a consonant, *w* appears before the vowel (*wagon*). As a vowel, *w* occurs after the vowel (*snow*). The *w* is silent before *r* (*write*). *W* may also be part of a blend (*dwell*) or a digraph (*what*). Occasionally, the letter *w* fools us. It appears to be part of the digraph *wh,* but is actually silent (*who*).

Xx does not have a key symbol. It may represent /ks/ (*six*), /gz/ (*exam*), or */z/* (*xylophone*). We are more apt to use /gz/ when *x* appears between two vowel phonemes (*exempt*).

Yy serves as a consonant and as a vowel. The *y* at the beginning of a syllable acts as a consonant and represents /y/ (*yellow*). *Y* within a syllable or at the end of a syllable acts as a vowel and may be silent (*play*), or may represent a vowel sound (*rhyme*).

Review 7

1. There are three consonants which, as single letters, represent no distinctive phonemes:
   a. The *c* usually represents the sound we associate with *s* when followed by

      _____ , _____ , or _____ .

      The *c* usually represents the sound we associate with _____ when

      followed by the vowels _____ , _____ , or _____ , most other consonants, or when appearing at the end of a word.
   b. The *q* always represents the sound we associate with _____ .
   c. The *x* can adequately be represented by the consonants_____ , _____ ,

      and _____ .
2. There are other letters which represent two or more sounds, one of which is the sound we commonly associate with that particular letter (key symbol).
   a. The *g* represents "its own sound," /*g*/, (the _____________ sound)
      (hard, soft)

      when followed by the vowels _____ , _____ , _____ , or by other consonants, or appears at the end of a word.
   b. The *g* usually represents its _____________ sound, that which we
      (hard, soft)

      ordinarily associate with the letter _____ , when followed by _____ ,

      _____ , or _____ .
3. The two most common sounds represented by the single letter *s* are:
   a. The sound we ordinarily associate with the letter *s,* as in

      _____________ .
      (some, sugar)
   b. The sound we ordinarily associate with the letter _____ , as in *hi<u>s</u>.*
4. The letter *d* may represent the sound we associate with _____ or with _____ when it appears in the suffix *-ed.*
5. *F* occasionally represents the sound we associate with _____ , as in *of.*
6. *T* in combination with a vowel may represent different sounds as _____ in

   question and _____ in *patient.*

7. Generalizations:
   a. Consonant letters may represent more than one sound.

      The *s* represents the sound of _____ (as the key symbol indicates), of _____ (*sure*), of _____ (*has*), and of _____ (*treasure*).

      The *z* represents the sound of _____ (as the key symbol indicates), of _____ (*quartz*), and of _____ (*azure*).
   b. Consonant sounds may be represented by more than one letter. The sound we hear at the beginning of *say* is often represented by *s,* by _____ (*cent*), or by _____ (*chintz*).
      The sound we hear at the beginning of the word *zipper* is sometimes represented by the letters _____ and _____ .
   c. Consonant letters may represent no sound. The three consonant letters that represent no sound in *knight* are _____ , _____ , and _____ . We call them ______________ letters. The letter _____ is ______________ in *soften, ballet,* and *latch.*
8. Reread the generalizations in question 7. Be sure you determine the difference between them. These generalizations would carry more precise meanings if the words *phoneme* and *grapheme* were used. Then they would read:
   a. Consonant ______________ may represent more than one ______________ .
   b. Consonant ______________ may be represented by more than one ______________ .
   c. Consonant letters may represent no ______________ .

   (See the Answers section for the answers to Review 7.)

Consonant Digraphs

26

vowels, 21

Three

18

1. We have been relating each of the consonant phonemes to its respective consonant letter.

There are _____ letters in the alphabet.

Five are ______________, so there are ______________ consonant letters.

______________ of these have no distinctive phoneme of their own.

This leaves ______________ consonant letters, each of which has been assigned a key symbol so as to build up a one-to-one correspondence between symbol and phoneme.

7

2. Eighteen symbols, but 25 consonant sounds! Where do we find the _____ remaining symbols?

We use two-letter combinations called digraphs to stand for the 7 phonemes not represented by single letter graphemes.

---

no

no

3. The *ch* is one of the two-letter digraphs we will study. Pronounce *chair.* Does the *ch* in *chair* represent the sound we usually associate with the *c* in *cat?* ______________ (yes, no) Does the *h* represent the sound we usually associate with the *h* in *hat?* ______________ (yes, no) The digraphs represent unique phonemes. The phonemes do not represent the sound usually associated with either letter when it occurs alone.

---

ch	*ch*	*chair*
sh	*sh*	*shoe*
th	*th*	*thumb*
th	*t̸h*	*that*
wh	*wh*	*whale*
	zh	*treasure*
ng	*ng*	*king*

4. The key symbols that represent the seven missing phonemes are listed at the right. Fill in the missing items in the table: digraphs (1), key words (3). Select the key words from these: *shoe, whale, king, thumb, chair, treasure.* Pronounce aloud the word and phoneme each represents. Notice that each is a distinctive consonant sound not represented by any single letter in our alphabet.

1	2	3
_____	*ch*	_________
_____	*sh*	_________
_____	*th*	_________
_____	*t̸h*	*that*
_____	*wh*	_________
	zh	_________
_____	*ng*	_________

BOX 2.7

Too Many English Sounds, Too Few English Letters: The French Solution

History books tell us that the French-speaking Normans ruled England from 1066 to roughly 1500 A.D. French became the language of the government, and hordes of French-speaking scribes were moved to England to keep the official records. The Norman French scribes were relatively unfamiliar with the English language. When the scribes realized that there were not enough English letters to represent the sounds in English words, they turned to the French writing system for a solution, introducing the *ch, sh, wh,* and *th* digraphs to represent the /ch/, /sh/, /wh/, voiced /th̸/, and unvoiced /th/. Let us consider why the Norman French scribes chose these particular two-letter combinations.

In Old French, the letter *h* was occasionally used to signal when the preceding consonant had an atypical pronunciation. When the French-speaking scribes wanted to represent the English /ch/, they used the *h* in English just as it had been used in Old French—to mark the unexpected pronunciation of the consonant letter. This is the reason why the *ch* digraph is spelled with a *c+h.* Following the same line of reasoning, the scribes used the letter *h* to alert the reader to the unexpected pronunciation of *s* when the /sh/ phoneme occurs in English words. The *sh* digraph reliably represents /sh/, except in French loan words in which the Norman scribes used the *ch* digraph to represent /sh/ (*machine, chivalry, chef, sachet*).

In Old English spelling, the *wh* in *when* was written as *hw.* The French-speaking scribes reversed the letters, thereby introducing the *wh* digraph. Say *when.* Do you hear /hw/? The Old English *hw* letter sequence is a more accurate description of English pronunciation. Modern dictionaries use the Old English letter sequence—*hw*—to record the pronunciation of the *wh* digraph in words such as *hwen, hwite,* and *hwisper.*

Old English used two letters, the *thorn* and the *edh,* to record the voiced *th̸* (*this*) and the unvoiced *th* (*thumb*). These two Old English letters were used interchangeably, so the reader did not know whether to use the voiced or unvoiced pronunciation. The Norman French scribes preferred the *th* digraph, and used it to represent both the voiced and unvoiced phonemes. Eventually, both the *thorn* and the *edh* disappeared from the English alphabet. In the Middle English period, after the Old English *thorn* had dropped from the alphabet, the letter *y* was occasionally used to represent /th/ in the initial position. How would you pronounce, "Ye Olde Malt Shoppe," in modern English? (If you said, "The Old Malt Shop," you are right! In the word *ye,* the letter *y* represents the /th/!)

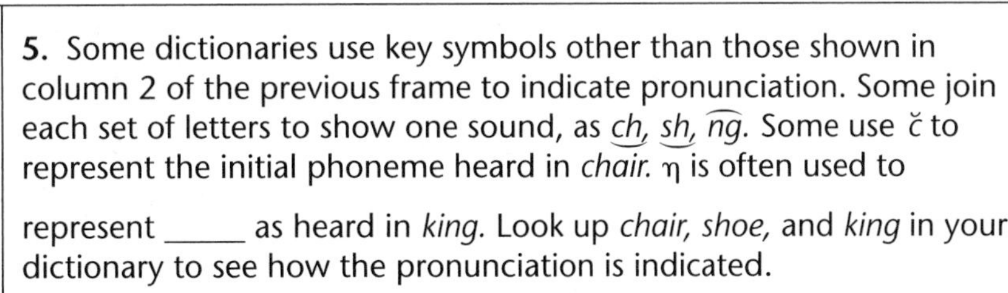

	5. Some dictionaries use key symbols other than those shown in column 2 of the previous frame to indicate pronunciation. Some join each set of letters to show one sound, as *ch͜, sh͜, n͡g.* Some use č to represent the initial phoneme heard in *chair.* ŋ is often used to
ng	represent _____ as heard in *king.* Look up *chair, shoe,* and *king* in your dictionary to see how the pronunciation is indicated.

	6. There are other consonant digraphs as *ph* and *gh*. However, they are not listed in frame 3 because they are already represented. The
f	key symbol _____ indicates the sound of the *ph* and the *gh*.

Review 8

Check yourself: Are you writing every answer and finishing each frame before moving the mask down? Are you getting almost every answer correct? Do you study more carefully when you miss one? Do you analyze your errors? Can you give yourself 100 on each review?

1. A grapheme composed of two letters that represent a single sound is called a ______________ .
2. Indicate the pronunciation of the underlined parts of the following words by using key symbols:

   quick *who* *measure* *whether* *which* *both*
   weather *notion* *sugar* *wish* *vision* *strong*
3. In the following words, underline all the consonant digraphs that serve as key symbols and cannot be replaced by a single letter from our alphabet:

   weather *enough* *whom* *which* *belong*
   wrist *wish* *both* *through* *condemn*
4. There are 25 consonant sounds in the American-English language. We identify 18 of them with single ______________ symbols. We should have ______________ more consonant letters in the alphabet. Since we do not, we use two-letter combinations called ______________ to serve as key symbols for these phonemes. Write the seven two-letter symbols. ___________
5. Our sound-symbol system is complicated by the use of other consonant digraphs standing for phonemes already represented in the system. Select three examples of such digraphs from these words:

   tough, chalk, sheath, short-sighted, chloroform, phoneme
6. These three digraphs are already represented by (use key symbols) _____ , _____ , _____ .
7. Rewrite these words using the appropriate key symbols for the consonants. Copy the vowels as they are.

   sunk *photograph* *know* *alphabet* *pheasant* *cough*

(See the Answers section for the answers to Review 8.)

ch, sh, zh

ch	**1.** We have no single letter in the alphabet to represent the first phoneme we hear in the key word *chair.* We will use the logical two-letter combination, the _____ , to identify this phoneme. Study the digraphs in these sets of words: 1 — *chair*, *chalk*, *churn* 2 — *character*, *chord*, *chaos* 3 — *chiffon*, *machine*, *chute*
no no	Each word contains the grapheme *ch.* Does each grapheme represent the phoneme we associate with the key symbol *ch?* _____ Try pronouncing each one using the first phoneme in *chair* for each digraph. Is the digraph *ch* reliable? _____
ch k If you guessed *sh,* you are right!	**2.** The digraph in each of the words in set 1 represents the phoneme we associate with the key symbol _____ . The digraphs in set 2 represent the phoneme we associate with the key symbol _____ . Can you guess what key symbol represents the digraphs in set 3? _____
no ch, k, sh	**3.** Is the digraph *ch* reliable as to the phoneme it represents? _____ If we do not know the word, we cannot tell which key symbol to identify with it. It might be _____ , or _____ , or _____ . (However, if you are an expert on language derivation, you will have clues.)
shoe	**4.** The sound heard at the beginning of *shoe* is very common, but there is no letter in the alphabet to represent it. We shall use the key symbol *sh* to represent the phoneme as heard in the key word _____________ . (*shoe, clip*)

one no	**5.** When *s* and *h* appear together in this order in a syllable, we expect them to represent ____________ phoneme(s). Can you hear the (How many?) separate phonemes represented by *s* and *h* in *shut?* ____________ If you could, you would hear the word *hut* in *shut.*
/*sh*/ *shure, ship, moshon, shugar, mashine, speshal*	**6.** *Sh* is very reliable in that when we see *sh,* we can be sure we will hear / /. However, the phoneme we represent by *sh* has a variety of graphemes; that is, it is spelled in a variety of ways. Examine the words below. Look at the underlined parts. Rewrite the words using *sh* to represent the underlined graphemes. *sure* ____________ *ship* ____________ *motion* ____________ *sugar* ____________ *machine* ____________ *special* ____________
s, sh, ti *s, ch, ci*	**7.** The graphemes that we associate with the key symbol *sh* are: ____ in *sure* ____ in *ship* ____ in *motion* ____ in *sugar* ____ in *machine* ____ in *special*
no	**8.** Now listen for the middle consonant sound as you say *treasure.* Is there a letter in the alphabet to represent this sound? ____
zh	**9.** We shall use the digraph *zh* as the key symbol to represent the phoneme heard in the key word *treasure,* although it is never represented in a word with the grapheme ____ .
pleazhure *vizhon* *sabotazhe* *azhure* *pich*	**10.** Rewrite the words at the right to indicate, by using the key symbols, the sounds of the underlined letters. *pleasure* ____________ *vision* ____________ *sabotage* ____________ *azure* ____________ *pitch* ____________
seizure *dozen*	**11.** The *z* occasionally stands for the /zh/ as in ____________ . (*seizure, dozen*) Pronounce *seizure* and *dozen* aloud. Which has the phoneme you hear in *zipper?* ____________

leisure, collage *treasure* do not	**12.** The *s* and *g* are two other graphemes which occasionally represent the /zh/ as in ________ (*leisure, base*) and ________ (*collage, age*). The *s* in the key word ________ (*treasure, sun*) represents the /zh/ phoneme. We ________ (do, do not) have a grapheme to represent the /zh/ phoneme.
decision *seizure* *beige* *garage* *measure*	**13.** Check the words at the right in which the underlined grapheme represents the /zh/. If you identify all of the words in which the /zh/ phoneme occurs, you are really thinking! *decision* *seizure* *beige* *garage* *person* *measure*
s, g	**14.** What letter represents the sound we associate with *zh* in *measure?* ____ In *rouge?* ____
never	**15.** *Zh* ________ (never, seldom) appears in a word, so it is not appropriate to make a statement regarding reliability.

Review 9

1. Use the key symbol to indicate the sound of each consonant in the following words. Underline the digraphs that represent distinctive phonemes.

a. *shiver*	**b.** *eggs*	**c.** *sure*	**d.** *share*
e. *treasure*	**f.** *character*	**g.** *brazier*	**h.** *Christmas*
i. *schools*	**j.** *ghosts*	**k.** *charge*	**l.** *chute*
m. *quack*	**n.** *lotion*	**o.** *division*	**p.** *Chicago*
q. *string*			

2. How does the *zh* differ from the other digraphs?

(See the Answers section for the answers to Review 9.)

th, t̸h, wh

no, no	**1.** Listen to the first phoneme while you pronounce *that* aloud. Compare it with the first phoneme in *thumb.* Do you hear the /*t*/ in either phoneme? ____________ the /*h*/? ____________
voiced	**2.** The /*th*/ heard in *thumb* is a whispered sound, a "voiceless" sound. On the other hand, we use our vocal cords when we say the first phoneme in *that.* We call it a ____________ phoneme. (voiced, voiceless)
there *think* *these* *thick* *those* *thing* *this* *thank*	**3.** You have learned that the *th* digraph represents two phonemes. One phoneme is voiced (*that*), the other phoneme is voiceless (*thumb*). A voiced phoneme is produced when the vocal cords vibrate. A voiceless phoneme is produced when the vocal cords do not vibrate. Pronounce the words at the right. Write the words in which the *th* is voiced in Column 1 below. Write the words in which the *th* is voiceless in Column 2. *think* *there* *thick* *these* *those* *thing* *this* *thank* Column 1 Voiced ____________ ____________ ____________ ____________ Column 2 Voiceless ____________ ____________ ____________ ____________
thorn	**4.** You must say these words aloud or you will not hear the voiced quality. Note that the voiceless phoneme has a whispered sound even when you say it aloud. The *th* in ____________ has a whispered or voiceless sound. Our (*this, thorn*) vocal cords do not vibrate.

Answer	Frame
think *thought* *thank* *through* *length* *both*	**5.** Many people do not realize that *th* is a grapheme which represents two sounds just as different as the sounds represented by *p* and *b* or *s* and *z.* They automatically use the correct sound for the words they have heard before. Check the words at the right in which the *th* represents the voiceless phoneme. You will not be able to tell the difference if you do not say them out loud! *think* *the* *though* *thought* *them* *they* *thank* *through* *length* *both*
toge~~th~~er, think, throw	**6.** Repeat all the words in the previous frame in which the *th* represents the voiceless phoneme. Then say all the words in which the *th* represents the voiced phoneme. We shall use ~~*th*~~ as the key symbol to represent the voiced sound. We shall use *th* as the key symbol to represent the voiceless sound. Rewrite the following words; underline the digraphs that represent the voiceless phonemes and put a slash through the digraphs that represent the voiced phoneme. *together* ____________ *think* ____________ *throw* ____________
phoneme voiced *their*	**7.** When we see an unknown word in our reading that contains the digraph *th,* we have no way of knowing which ____________ it represents. We can use the dictionary. Many dictionaries use the slash to indicate that the *th* represents the v____________ phoneme as in ____________ . (*their, worth*)

the *bath, /t/*	**8.** The *th* is not a reliable digraph. It may represent the voiced sound heard in ____________ , the voiceless sound heard in (*the, third*) ____________ , or, in rare instances, the / / as in *Thomas.* (*bath, bathe*)
wh *what*	**9.** Another phoneme composed of two letters is ____________ as heard in *whale.* It is also heard in ____________ . (*who, what*)
w You are correct, whatever your response.	**10.** This phoneme may give you some trouble because it is rapidly disappearing from our language. If you pronounce *weather* and *whether* exactly the same, you are following the trend in America. Many people make the phoneme represented by the key symbol *wh* sound like that represented by the single letter _____ . What do you do? Pronounce *whistle, white.* Do they sound like *wistle, wite?* ____________
wh *while*	**11.** Most dictionaries note this trend but continue to indicate the pronunciation of words beginning with *wh* as *hw.* We will use the key symbol _____ to represent the sound of the digraph, although it actually is better represented by *hw.* *Wh* represents the phoneme heard in ____________ . (Pronounce (*whom, while*) *whom* and *while* carefully so that you will hear the distinction.)
beginning	**12.** The *wh,* like the consonant *w,* appears at the ____________ of the word or syllable and is followed by a vowel.

BOX 2.8

When Is a Bumkin a Pumpkin?

An Easy Way to Recognize Voiced and Voiceless Phonemes and Some Insight into Invented Spelling

You have learned that your vocal cords vibrate when pronouncing voiced phonemes, and do not vibrate when pronouncing voiceless phonemes. However, sometimes it is difficult to determine from listening alone whether a particular phoneme is voiced or voiceless. To identify a voiced phoneme, you must find your voice. Here is a quick and easy way to do this:

1. Lightly place your hand over the lower part of your throat.
2. Pronounce each pair of words below:

   zap sap   *ban pan*   *den ten*   *gin kin*   *van fan*

3. Now pronounce each pair again, only this time draw out the phoneme that is represented by the underlined grapheme. When exaggerating the pronunciation of the phoneme, pay special attention to the vibration of your vocal cords. When you feel your vocal cords vibrate, you have found your voice, and you have also identified a voiced phoneme! Which phoneme in each word pair is voiced? Which is voiceless? (See answers below.)
4. To put this into a useful context for the teaching of reading, pronounce each pair once again, this time paying special attention to the way in which you form (articulate) each voiced and voiceless phoneme. Concentrate on your tongue, teeth, and lips. What do you notice about the way in which you articulate each voiced and voiceless phoneme pair?

   If you noticed that the phonemes in each pair represent the same articulation, and differ only in the presence or the absence of breath, you are very observant!

Understanding the voiced and voiceless phoneme pairs will help you to interpret children's misspellings. Sometimes, as children spell, they confuse phonemes that have the same articulation but differ in voicing. Suppose a child writes *bumkin* for *pumpkin.* This misspelling might be due to insufficient phonics knowledge, or to misperceiving the letters *b* and *p.* There is, however, another explanation: Perhaps the child, when thinking about the sounds of the English language, confused the /b/ and /p/ phonemes. After all, these phonemes are articulated in the same manner, and only differ in their voiced and voiceless qualities. Understanding the voiced and voiceless phonemes helps you, the teacher, recognize the many ways in which children combine their knowledge of the phonemes of the English language with their knowledge of phonics in order to spell words when writing.

Answer to step 3: If you said that the voiced phonemes are /z/, /b/, /d/, /g/, and /v/, you are right!

Review 10

1. We have identified each of the seven graphemes that serve as additions to our alphabet. Six of them are contained in the words below. Write the key symbol following the word in which each is found.

swing	_____	*white*	_____	*measure*	_____
mother	_____	*flash*	_____	*porch*	_____

2. One grapheme is missing from the group of digraphs above.

   It is found in ______________ .
   (*breath, breathe*)

3. We have identified all 18 single letter phonemes. They are heard in the initial position in each of the following words: *boat, dog, fish, goat, hat, jeep, kite, lion, moon, nut, pig, ring, sun, table, van, wagon, yo-yo, zipper.* Select key words from those above to illustrate phonemes represented by the underlined graphemes in the following words. Those that have no key word may be left blank.

   Examples: *work* *wagon* *psychology* _____

(1) *could*	______________	(9) *of*	______________
(2) *yonder*	______________	(10) *get*	______________
(3) *circle*	______________	(11) *honor*	______________
(4) *jumped*	______________	(12) *tall*	______________
(5) *gist*	______________	(13) *my*	______________
(6) *bomb*	______________	(14) *wrong*	______________
(7) *palm*	______________	(15) *little*	______________
(8) *ghetto*	______________	(16) *rag*	______________

4. The word *gem* ______________ a key word because the *g* ______________ represent the phoneme we associate with the key symbol *g*.
   (is, is not) (does, does not)

5. The word *try* is not a key word for the *y* phoneme because the *y* is not at the beginning of the syllable; it is, therefore, not a ______________ letter.
   (consonant, vowel)

6. From the following words, select those that contain the /t̸h/ phoneme:

path	*thorn*	*write*	*wheel*
white	*theme*	*this*	*author*
father	*whip*	*mouth*	*cloth*
wrong	*feather*	*them*	*whistle*

7. Which of the words in question 6 contain the /*wh*/ phoneme?
8. What do the consonants *w* and *wh* have in common?

(See the Answers section for the answers to Review 10.)

ng

Answers	Frame
beginning follows	**1.** The phoneme /*ng*/ is different from the others represented by digraphs in that it is never heard at the _____________ of a syllable, (beginning, ending) or, to put it another way, it always _____________ the vowel. (precedes, follows)
baŋ yes *ranjer* no *stuŋ* *hinj* *briŋiŋ*	**2.** Say the words at the right aloud. Does each contain the letters *ng?* _____ Does each contain the digraph *ng?* _____ Rewrite the words to show pronunciation of the consonants. (Copy the vowels, omit silent *e*). In this set, use *ŋ* to represent the *ng* digraph. *bang* _____________ *ranger* _____________ *stung* _____________ *hinge* _____________ *bringing* _____________
/*ng*/ *sing* *pingk* *blangk* *fingger* *jinjer* *singk* *trianggle*	**3.** Recall that *n* generally represents / / when followed by *g* or *k*. Rewrite these words, indicating pronunciation of the consonants. Use *ng* (but underline it) to represent the digraph. Work carefully. This takes a keen ear. *sing* _____________ *pink* _____________ *blank* _____________ *finger* _____________ *ginger* _____________ *sink* _____________ *triangle* _____________

finger, triangle	**4.** In which words from the preceding frame do you hear hard *g*, /*g*/, as well as /*ng*/?
digraph *gingham* *orange*	**5.** The letters *n* and *g* together in a word are most commonly a ______________, that is, a two-letter combination representing a single phoneme as in ______________ (*gingham, ungrateful*). However, they may represent two separate phonemes as in ______________ (*orange, among*).
digraphs *chair* *sh* *zh* *th* *that* *whale* *ng*	**6.** We have identified the seven ______________ that represent distinct phonemes not represented by the single letters in the alphabet. They are (1) *ch* as in ______________ (*chair, choir*) (2) _____ as in *shoe* (3) _____ sounded like the *s* in *treasure* (4) _____ as in *thumb* (5) *t̸h* as in ______________ (*that, thrill*) (6) *wh* as in ______________ (*whole, whale*) (7) _____ as in *king*

BOX 2.9

Consonant Digraph Study Guide

ch, sh, th, wh, ng

Digraph	Key Symbol	Key Word
ch	*ch*	*chair*
sh	*sh*	*shoe*
th	*th*	*thumb*
th	*t̸h*	*that*
wh	*wh*	*whale*
	zh	*treasure*
ng	*ng*	*king*

The consonant digraphs are two-letter combinations which represent unique phonemes. The phonemes which the digraphs represent are different from the sounds associated with either of the two consonant letters when they occur alone in words.

ch The digraph *ch* is not reliable. *Ch* may represent the /ch/ (*chair*), the /k/ (*character*), or the /sh/ (*machine*).

sh The /sh/ is a very common sound in the English language. The *sh* (*shoe*) is very reliable.

Voiceless th The digraph *th* represents two distinct phonemes, one voiceless and one voiced. The /th/ in the key word *thumb* is a whispered sound, which we call the voiceless *th* (*thorn, thick*).

Voiced t̸h We use our vocal cords to pronounce the /th/ phoneme in the key word *that,* which we refer to as the voiced *t̸h* (*there, father*). Dictionaries may use a slash, a line, or italics to indicate the voiced digraph *t̸h* (*t̸h,* th, *th*). We will use the slash (t̸h) as the key symbol.

wh The digraph *wh* represents /hw/ (*why, white*). *Wh* occurs in the beginning of syllables, and is followed by a vowel.

zh While /zh/ occurs in English words (*measure, vision*), the /zh/ is never represented in a word with the grapheme *zh.* The /zh/ may be represented by the *s* (*pleasure, vision*), the *g* (*collage*) or the *z* (*seizure*).

ng The digraph *ng* is never heard at the beginning of a syllable, and always follows a vowel. The letters *ng* may represent /ng/ (*sing, among*). The letter *n* may also represent /ng/ when it is followed by the letter *g* (*finger—fing-ger*) or the letter *k* (*pink—pingk*). Your dictionary may use the symbol ŋ to represent /ng/.

Review 11

1. Which of the seven representative digraphs never appears at the beginning of a word?
2. Rewrite these words showing consonant pronunciation. (This calls for acute hearing.)

   Underline the digraphs. Pronounce vowels as you would in the actual word.

   a. *mango, manger, mangy*
   b. *pin, ping, pink, ping-pong*
   c. *ban, bang, bank, banking*
   d. *ran, rang, rank, ranking*
   e. *rancher, range, fancy*
3. There are 25 consonant sounds in the American-English language.

   a. We identify 18 of them with single letter symbols. Write the 18 consonant letters. ______________

   b. We use ______________ to identify the seven additional phonemes. Write the seven digraphs. ______________
4. *C* was not included in question 3.a. because ______________ .
5. What other consonant letters were not included?
6. The digraph *ph* was not included in question 3.b. because ______________ .
7. Rewrite the following words using appropriate key symbols for the consonants. Omit silent consonants. Copy vowels as they are.

whole	_____	*high*	_____
quick	_____	*gopher*	_____
wholly	_____	*phone*	_____
thatch	_____	*that*	_____
taught	_____	*comb*	_____
glistening	_____	*daughter*	_____
rustle	_____	*doubt*	_____
knot	_____	*budget*	_____
wrap	_____	*thinking*	_____

(See the Answers section for the answers to Review 11.)

Consonant Clusters and Blends

Answers	Frames
letters, digraphs *bl*	**1.** We have identified each of the 25 consonant phonemes of the American-English language: 18 of these are represented by single ____________ ; 7 are represented by ____________ . Now let us turn our attention to consonants that form a cluster in a word. What **cluster** of consonant letters do you see in the word *blue?* ____
2 *b, l*	**2.** Pronounce the word *blue.* How many consonant phonemes does *blue* contain? ____ What are they? ____ ____
one **clusters**	**3.** A digraph is a two-letter grapheme that represents ____________ speech sound. The word *blue* does not contain a consonant digraph. Neither the *b* nor the *l* loses its identity. Both are sounded, but they are blended together. We call such combinations of consonant letters ____________ , and the sounds they represent we call **blends.** We need to study the consonant blends because in many ways they act as one phoneme.
bl, cl, fl, dr ft *sk, fr, spr, spl* *Sh is a digraph.* *k*	**4.** **A consonant cluster is composed of two or more consonants which blend together when sounded to form a consonant blend.** The letters do not form a digraph. The phonemes in the blend retain their individual identity. Pronounce the words below. Fill in the blanks with the letters that form the consonant clusters. *black* ____ *clown* ____ *flying* ____ *draft* ____ *desk* ____ *fry* ____ *spray* ____ *splash* ____ Why did you omit the *sh* in *splash?* ____________________ The *ck* in *black* represents the single consonant ____ , not a blend.
s p l, blends	**5.** Some reading series do not use the term *cluster.* In that case, *blend* refers to both letters and sounds. In the word *splash,* for example, the letters ____ ____ ____ as well as /*spl*/ are called ____________ .

1. *r* 2. *l* 3. *s*	**6.** Pronounce the words in each set below. Each set has one of the common "blenders." Write the letter common to each consonant cluster in the set. 1: *brown*, *street*, *great* ____ 2: *flame*, *claim*, *split* ____ 3: *skate*, *snow*, *street* ____
r, *l*, *s*	**7.** The common blenders are represented by the letters _____, _____, and _____. However, there are clusters that do not contain these letters.
cluster digraph *sh* *ch* *th*	**8.** We distinguish a ______________ from a digraph by the fact that it represents two or more phonemes blended together. The ______________ represents a single sound. Check those combinations in the following list which do <u>not</u> represent consonant blends. *bl* *cr* *qu* *sc* *scr* *cl* *dr* *tw* *sh* *spr* *gl* *sk* *ch* *sm* *spl* *sl* *pr* *th* *mp* *str*
w *equal, quart, queen, quick*	**9.** It may seem strange to classify *qu* as a consonant cluster when *u* is a vowel. The *u* in this case, however, takes the sound of the consonant _____. So this combination is actually a /*kw*/ <u>blend.</u> Select the words with the /*kw*/ blend from the following: *equal* *quart* *unique* *queen* *opaque* *quick*
tr, tw, gr, spl, qu *pl, str, sl, pr, gr-sp* (<u>NOT</u> *ch* or *sh!*)	**10.** Underline the consonant clusters in these words: *tree* *twin* *great* *splash* *chair* *quilt* *please* *she* *street* *slow* *pretty* *grasp*
s, *h*	**11.** The *sh* in *splash* and the *sh* in *she* cannot be blends because the sounds represented by the _____ and the _____ are not heard.

Answers	Frame
field *lamp* *bent* *task* *fast* *hand* *belt* *draft*	**12.** Many consonant clusters occur in the final position in English words or syllables. Read the words at the right. Underline the consonant clusters that occur at the end of the words. *field* *dish* *lamp* *bent* *task* *fast* *hand* *church* *belt* *draft*
train *task*	**13.** As you have seen, clusters may appear at the beginning of a word or syllable, as in *train,* or at the end of a word or syllable, as in *task.* Underline the appropriate blend in both of these examples.
Clusters / *Digraphs* *speech* / *speech* *rest* / *church* *digraph* / *digraph* *trash* / *trash* *shield* / *shield*	**14.** Arrange the words below in two columns: those with clusters representing blends and those with digraphs. Some words may be used in both columns. Underline to indicate the part in each word that qualifies it to be in the particular column. Clusters — Digraphs *speech, church, rest, digraph, trash, shield*
t, h, *r, th*	**15.** There are many words in which a consonant digraph is a part of a cluster. Examine the word *throw.* The first three letters: _____ , _____ , and _____ compose a cluster. Within the cluster is the digraph _____ . All blend together: /*thr*/.
thr shr chr phr *ch ph*	**16.** Draw a single line under the digraph, and another line under the entire cluster in these words: *through* *shrimp* *chrome* *phrase* Which of the digraphs in the above words are not one of the seven key symbols needed to complete the phonemes of our language? _____ _____

Answer	Frame
str, str ngth, scr *bl nd, sm, thr ft*	**17.** All consonant clusters (written) represent blends (spoken). Underline the consonants that represent blends in these words: *string* *strength* *scrap* *blond* *small* *thrift*
strength */ng/* and */th/*	**18.** Which word in frame 17 has a cluster composed of two digraphs? ____________ The two digraphs which blend together are / / and / /.
Blends: *toast*, *grapheme*, *three*, *clanging*, *strike* Digraphs: *diphthong*, *grapheme*, *three*, *clanging*, *altogether*, *father*	**19.** Arrange the words below in two columns: those containing clusters that represent blends and those containing digraphs. Some of these words, too, may be used in both columns, so underline to indicate the part of each word that places it in a column. (Columns: Blends, Digraphs) *toast, diphthong, grapheme, three,* *clanging, strike, altogether, father*
phoneme	**20.** We have studied the single consonant phonemes, the consonant digraphs, and the consonant blends. We include the blends because in many ways, one blend acts as though it were one ____________ .

BOX 2.10

Consonant Clusters and Blends Study Guide

Consonant Clusters

A consonant cluster is composed of two or more consonants which blend together when sounded to form a consonant blend (*clown, spray*). Some teachers' manuals do not use the term *cluster.* In that case, *blend* refers to both letters and sounds. We will use the more frequently used term, *blend,* in this study guide.

Beginning Consonant Blends

The most common blends that occur at the beginning of a word or syllable include the letters *r, l,* and *s.*

r Blends		*l* Blends		*s* Blends			
br	*bright*	*bl*	*black*	*sc*	*scout*	*scr*	*scrap*
cr	*crayon*	*cl*	*class*	*sk*	*sky*	*spl*	*splash*
dr	*dress*	*fl*	*flower*	*sl*	*slip*	*spr*	*spring*
fr	*free*	*gl*	*glad*	*sm*	*small*	*squ*	*square*
gr	*green*	*pl*	*plan*	*sn*	*snow*	*str*	*string*
pr	*pretty*			*sp*	*spot*		
tr	*train*			*st*	*stop*		
				sw	*swim*		

tw and dw The *tw* (*twin*) and *dw* (*dwell*) blends are less common in English than the blends which include the letters *r, l,* or *s.*

qu *Qu* is a consonant blend when it represents /kw/ as in *quick* and *quilt.*

English syllables can have no more than three consonant letters in a single, beginning blend. Three-letter blends that represent three phonemes are *scl* (*sclerosis*), *scr* (*scrap*), *spr* (*spring*), and *str* (*street*).

Consonant blends are taught as units rather than as single graphemes (e.g., *st* as representing two blended phonemes rather than an isolated /s/ and an isolated /t/).

Consonant Digraphs and Consonant Blends

Blends that occur at the beginning of a syllable may include a consonant digraph and a consonant cluster, such as in *shr* (*shrimp*), and *thr* (*throw*).

Final Position Blends

Many consonant blends occur in the final position in English syllables. Some of the more common final blends include:*

ld	*old*	*nd*	*end*	*st*	*most*	*mp*	*lamp*	*lt*	*salt*
lk	*milk*	*nt*	*went*	*sk*	*desk*	*ft*	*lift*		

*In teaching, vowels may be combined with consonant blends to create letter patterns which we call rimes. You will learn about rimes in Part VI of this book. Examples of vowel and consonant blend rimes include *old* (*told*); *ild* (*wild*); *ilk* (*milk*); *alt* (*salt*); *end* (*mend*); *ent* (*went*); *ost* (*most*); *esk* (*desk*); *amp* (*lamp*); *ift* (*lift*).

Review 12

1. A cluster differs from a digraph in that ______________.
2. Why were no key symbols given to represent the blends?
3. Seven specific digraphs together with 18 single letters supply us with the consonant sounds of our language. Which of the seven digraphs appear in the following paragraph? List them in the order in which they make their first appearance.

   It started as a pleasure trip. The driver, nearing the exit leading through the city, changed lanes. He jerked the wheel too quickly and landed on the slick shoulder.

4. There are three unnecessary single letters in our alphabet. Illustrations are in the above paragraph. Rewrite these words to show how other letters could substitute.
5. What consonant blends are heard at the beginning of words in the above paragraph?

(See the Answers section for the answers to Review 12.)

For a helpful summary and review of the phonemes, turn to page 151. Work through the consonant section, using a separate sheet of paper. Then you will be able to have a complete review after you have studied the vowels.

Recap I

25 phonemes word	**1.** In our study of consonants, we identified ______ consonant ______________ (the smallest unit of sound that distinguishes one ______________ from another).
symbol *b d f g h j k l m n p* *r s t v w y z* digraphs *ch sh th t̸h wh zh ng*	**2.** To know exactly to which sound we are referring, we assigned each phoneme a key ______________ and a key word. As you go through the alphabet, write the 18 consonant letters that symbolize specific phonemes: ____ ____ ____ ____ ____ ____ ____ ____ ____ ____ ____ ____ ____ ____ ____ ____ ____ ____. But we need 25 symbols. We use ____________ to complete our representation of the consonant phonemes: ____ ____ ____ ____ ____ ____ ____.

phoneme	**3.** Although consonants are fairly reliable (there is a high relationship between grapheme and ____________), there are irregularities:
phoneme	1. A letter (or grapheme) may represent more than one ____________. For example:
/k/ /s/	the c in *camp* represents / /, and in *ace* / /
/d/ /t/	the d in *date* / /, and in *jumped* / /
/j/ /g/	the g in *age* / /, and in *go* / /
/n/ /ng/	the n in *ran* / /, and in *rank* / /
/s/ /sh/ /z/ /zh/	the s in *soap* / /, in *surely* / /, in *runs* / / and in *measure* / /
/s/ /z/ /zh/	the z in *waltz* / /, in *quiz* / /, and in *azure* / /
/f/ *face, lauf, fone*	**4.** A phoneme may be represented by more than one grapheme. Write the phoneme which is represented in each set of words. Then rewrite the words, using the key symbols. (frames 4 and 5) / / as in *face* ________, *laugh* ________, *phone* ________
/j/ *page, joke,* *fuje, grajual* /k/ *ankor, antikue* *kue* /z/ *uzed, frozen,* *zylophone*	**5.** / / *page* ____________, *joke* ____________ *fudge* ____________, gra*d*ual ____________ / / *anchor* ____________, *antique* ____________, *cue* ____________ / / *used* ____________, *frozen* ____________, xylophone ____________
silent t s b k h	**6.** 3. A letter may represent no phoneme: it may be ____________. Some common silent letter patterns are: The second of two like-consonants, as the ______ in *letters,* the ______ in *dress* ______ following *m,* as in *bomb;* followed by *t* as in *doubt* ______ followed by *n,* as in *know* ______ following *g,* as in *ghost*

Use your dictionary to verify.	**7.** Did you feel there were any words which did not belong in the last 4 frames, words you would pronounce in a different way? List them here:
girl *give*	**8.** Repeat the generalization regarding the hard-soft sounds of c and g. Check the following words that do not follow the generalization. *music* *gem* *ghost* *girl* *comic* *success* *cycle* *give*
before F	**9.** The consonants *w* and *y* are found __________ (before, after) the vowel in a word. The consonant *y* is often a silent letter. T F
k	**10.** The key symbol for *q* is k.
I hope so. That would be a real achievement.	**11.** Did you get all the exercises in this recap correct? What a sense of satisfaction you must have. Congratulations! We have been studying the consonants, the most regular of all the phonemes. But the consonants cannot get along without the vowels. We will now proceed with a study of the vowels and their relationships with the consonants.

Part III

Vowels

A reminder: Do not pull the mask down until you have written your response to the entire frame.

vowels	**1.** The 26 letters of the alphabet are divided into two major categories: consonants and ____________ .
phonemes phonemes, 19 phonemes	**2.** Although there are many variations due to dialect, individual speech patterns, etc., for all practical purposes in the task of teaching reading we can consider the American-English language to contain 44 separate and distinctive ____________ . We have noted that 25 of these are consonant ____________ . Therefore, there are ____________ vowel ____________
vowels	**3.** **The letters *a, e, i, o, u,* and sometimes *w* and *y* are classified as ____________ .**
yo-yo	**4.** How can you tell when *y* is a consonant and when it is a vowel? You have learned that the key symbol *y* (consonant) represents the phoneme heard in ____________ (*yo-yo, say*). *Y* functions as a consonant <u>only</u> when it represents the phoneme heard in *yo-yo.*

initial	**5.** The consonant *y* is always the ____________ (initial, final) letter in a word or syllable. It is always found before the vowel.
consonant *yellow* *yet* vowel *beyond*	**6.** Study the words at the right. Underline each *y* that is a consonant. The ____________ (consonant, vowel) *y* is never a silent letter. The ____________ (consonant, vowel) *y* is often a silent letter. *they* *yellow* *yet* *may* *very* *beyond*
vowel	**7.** *Y* does not serve as a key symbol for a vowel phoneme. ***Y* represents no vowel sound of its own. When *y* is a ____________, its pronunciation is shown by the key symbols we associate with the *i* or the *e*.**
year (c) *gym* (v) *my* (v) *ready* (v) *canyon* *canyon* (c)	**8.** Study the function of the *y* in the words at the right. Place a c̲ or a v̲ above each *y* to identify *y* as a consonant or as a vowel. Check each *y* consonant to see that it represents the same sound as the initial phoneme in *yo-yo*. In which word is the *y* the first letter in the second syllable? ____________ *year* *gym* *my* *ready* *canyon*
wagon	**9.** Now let us examine the *w*. You have learned that *w* as a consonant represents the phoneme heard in ____________ (*wagon, snow*).
symbol	**10.** **As a vowel, the *w* represents no distinct phoneme of its own.** Therefore, it cannot be represented by a key ____________. ***W* is always used in combination with another vowel** as in *few, cow, grow.*

thaw, threw	**11.** Underline the ***w*** s that function as vowels in the following words: *water, which, thaw, threw, dwarf* (Be sure that they do not represent the phoneme you hear at the beginning of *wagon.*)
follows	The vowel *w* always ____________ another vowel. (precedes, follows)
w, y	**12.** Two of the seven vowels are not identified by distinctive key symbols because they do not represent sounds of their own. These are the vowels _____ and _____ .
a, e, i, o, u	**13.** Now let us turn our attention to the vowels that do represent phonemes and can be assigned key symbols to distinguish them from each other. The vowel phonemes are represented by five letters. They are _____ , _____ , _____ , _____ , _____ .
cannot be	**14.** These five vowels, alone and in combination with another vowel, represent the 19 vowel phonemes of our language. Therefore, there ____________ a one-to-one correspondence between phoneme and (is, cannot be) letter.
a 5	**15.** Study the words at the right. Pronounce the sound represented by the underlined vowel. We can see that one vowel, the _____ , represents at least _____ different phonemes. *same* *dare* *can* *arm* *about*
phoneme	**16.** Each vowel letter represents more than one ____________ . If we meet an unfamiliar word, how will we know which sounds its vowels represent?
vowels	There are some patterns (with exceptions, of course) which will give us some help in determining the sounds represented by the ____________ in unknown words.

phonemes vowel	**17.** Our task, then, is twofold: (1) To identify the vowel ____________ of the American-English language and assign each a key symbol. (2) To become acquainted with the generalizations that will aid us in associating the correct phonemes with the ____________ letters in unknown words.
letters	**18.** For our study, we shall divide the vowel phonemes into two major groups: (1) those represented by single vowel letters (2) those represented by combinations of vowel letters Each of the single letters (as in group 1) and each of the combinations of ____________ represent <u>one</u> phoneme.
letter	**19.** We shall begin our study of the vowel phonemes with group 1: those represented by a single vowel ____________ . (letter, phoneme)

Review 13

1. The vowel letters are ____, ____, ____, ____, ____, and sometimes ____ and ____ .
2. We need not select key symbols to represent the sounds of ____ and ____, because they duplicate the sounds of other vowels.
3. Indicate whether the *w* and the *y* in these words are consonants or vowels by writing <u>C</u> or <u>V</u> following each word:

yet	____	*type*	____	*play*	____
wide	____	*draw*	____	*when*	____

4. The *w* in *white* is part of a ____________ ____________ .
   (consonant, vowel) (blend, digraph)
5. There are ____________ vowel phonemes than there are vowel letters.
   (fewer, more)
6. How many vowel phonemes will we need to identify?

(See the Answers section for the answers to Review 13.)

Short Vowel Sounds

	ă (*apple*) ĕ (*elephant*) ĭ (*igloo*) ŏ (*ox*) ŭ (*umbrella*)
	1. One set of phonemes represented by single vowel letters includes those that stand for "short" vowel sounds. The **breve** is a diacritical mark used to indicate the specific pronunciation of each vowel in this group. Its linguistic relationship to "short" can be noted in such words as *abbreviate* and *brevity.* It is the custom, in phonics, to call the vowel sound whose key symbol contains a breve a **short** vowel sound.
a *ă* *ăpple* *e* *ĕ* *ĕlephant* *i* *ĭ* *ĭgloo* *o* *ŏ* *ŏx* *u* *ŭ* *ŭmbrella*	1 2 3 *a* *ă* *apple* *e* *ĕ* *elephant* *i* *ĭ* *igloo* *o* *ŏ* *ox* *u* *ŭ* *umbrella*
short breve	The vowels in column 3 at the right represent the ______________ sounds. Each key symbol (2) consists of the vowel marked with a ______________ .
	Mark the vowel in each key word.
short	**2.** Because, in actuality, these sounds are not held for a shorter period of time than certain other vowel phonemes, some prefer to call them **unglided phonemes.** If you write "unglided" and this text gives the answer as "______________" (or vice versa), you may count your answer correct.
ĭ, ŏ, ŭ phonemes	**3.** The key symbols that identify the vowels when they represent their short sounds are: *ă, ĕ,* _____ , _____ , _____ . Reading would be easier if five additional characters representing these ______________ (letters, phonemes) were added to our alphabet.
m *a,* consonant *p* *apple*	**4.** Pronounce the word *map.* Listen for three phonemes, the consonant phoneme represented by _____ , the vowel phoneme represented by _____ , and the ______________ phoneme represented by _____ . Pronounce the vowel sound alone. The same vowel sound is heard in ______________ (*apple, far*).

măp *map* *ran, grab, back*	**5.** Pronounce the vowel phoneme in *map.* Rewrite *map* using key symbols: ____________ . It is important to note that various dictionaries indicate pronunciation in different ways. We must study the pronunciation key of the particular dictionary we use. For example, many dictionaries indicate the pronunciation of all short vowel sounds with the letter and no diacritical mark. In these dictionaries, the pronunciation of *map* is written _____ . Pronounce the following words. Circle those whose vowel phoneme is the same as that in *map.* *ran all car above grab back paw*
3 *hĕn*	**6.** There are _____ phonemes in *hen.* Listen for the vowel phoneme as you say *hen* aloud. Rewrite *hen* using key symbols to indicate its pronunciation. ____________
mĕt, lĕg, ĕnd	**7.** Mark with a breve each of the vowels in the words below that represent the same vowel phoneme heard in the key word *elephant.* *feed met rib leg end reward* If you find this difficult, pronounce the first vowel phoneme heard in *elephant,* then pronounce each word, substituting that sound for each vowel phoneme.
3 *rĕd*	**8.** Read this sentence aloud: *I read a book yesterday.* How many phonemes do you hear when you say "read" in the sentence above? _____ Rewrite *read* using a key symbol to indicate each phoneme. ____________ You have written in code. Anyone who knows the code can pronounce *read* correctly without a sentence to clarify it.
pĭn, drĭp, lĭft, thĭk	**9.** Pronounce *igloo.* Now say the first vowel phoneme. Rewrite the following words using key symbols to code each phoneme: *pin* _____ *drip* _____ *lift* _____ *thick* _____
3 *ox*	**10.** Pronounce *hot.* It contains _____ phonemes. The vowel phoneme (How many?) sounds the same as that in ____________ . (*boy, ox*)

Answers	Frames
lĭp, tŏp, pŏp, *lăp, grăph, pŏd* key, symbols	**11.** Indicate the pronunciation of each short (unglided) vowel sound by using the correct diacritical mark in these words: *lip top note pop lap graph pod home* The vowel letters with the marks you placed above them are the ____________ ____________ for the phonemes they represent.
breve or *ŭ* *jŭmp, ŭs, dŭk, cŭp, tŭb*	**12.** Pronounce *umbrella.* We use the ____________ to indicate that the *u* represents a short (unglided) sound. Now, pronounce the vowel sound alone. Place the correct diacritical marks above all the vowels in the following words that represent the same sound as the first vowel phoneme in the key word *umbrella.* *jump use us duck cup house tub*
short *fĕnce* *dŭg*	**13.** Pronounce the vowel phoneme represented by the vowel letter in each of the words in column 1 at the right. Each vowel represents its ____________ phoneme. Now pronounce the vowel phoneme in each of the words in column 2. Place a breve above each vowel in column 2 that represents its unglided sound. Check carefully. 1: *an, fed, pin, hot, cup* 2: *car, fence, pine, cow, dug*
hĕd *sĕd* *sĕnts* *ĕnd*	**14.** Pronounce the words at the right. Listen carefully for the vowel phonemes. Rewrite each word, using the key symbols that indicate the sounds we associate with the vowel and consonant phonemes. *head* ____________ *said* ____________ *cents* ____________ *end* ____________
1 1 2 2 phoneme	**15.** To obtain a better understanding of the short vowels, we will consider them as they usually occur within the English syllable. A syllable is the smallest unit of speech which has one vowel phoneme. When you say the word *mat,* you hear ____________ (How many?) vowel phoneme(s). The word *mat* consists of ____________ (How many?) syllable(s). When you pronounce *mattress,* you hear ____________ (How many?) vowel phoneme(s). *Mattress* has ____________ (How many?) syllable(s). A syllable in the English language has only one vowel ____________ .

vowel, consonant	16. **The most common vowel-consonant pattern is that of CVC (consonant-vowel-consonant) in which the V (vowel) represents its short sound.** There are many one-syllable words and many accented syllables in multisyllable words which follow this pattern. These words and syllables are made of an initial consonant, a middle __________, and a final __________ .
ring, this, rab bit, big	**17.** The C (consonant) in the pattern may represent a digraph or a blend. Circle the syllables (or one-syllable words) that have the CVC pattern. *ring this rab bit be side rain big*
short (unglided) C	**18.** VC, in which the vowel represents the __________ sound as in *an,* is also a common pattern. It functions the same as the CV _____ pattern.
short (unglided) breve	19. **The CVC and the VC patterns give clues to the pronunciation of unknown words. In both cases we would expect the vowel to represent the __________ sound.** To indicate the pronunciation of the vowel, we place a __________ above it.
sĕt, lŏt yes (Blends and digraphs are considered as Cs.) no	**20.** Do the vowels in all CVC patterns represent the short sound? Study the following words and syllables. *far ther long set lot her* Do all of them have the CVC pattern? _____ Do all the vowels represent the short sound? _____ Mark the vowels that represent the short sounds with breves. Work carefully.
yes *Dăn kĕpt hĭs pŏp gŭn.*	**21.** The key words given at the beginning of this section will help us remember the phoneme for each vowel. A sentence that contains each of the short vowel phonemes may be easier to remember. Would the sentence below furnish a key word for each of the short vowel phonemes? __________ (Check each word with the set at the beginning of this section.) Mark the vowels with breves. *Dan kept his pop gun.*

4 *Năn's pĕt ĭs nŏt fŭn.* *Săm's nĕt ĭs nŏt cŭt.* *Săd Tĕd ĭn hŏt hŭt.* *All mĕn ĭn hŏt bŭs.*	**22.** Look at the groups of words below. Mark the vowels that represent the short sound. No. _____ is not a good key phrase. (1) *Nan's pet is not fun.* (2) *Sam's net is not cut.* (3) *Sad Ted in hot hut.* (4) *All men in hot bus.*
chim *men* *sun* *can* *win* *wish* *gin*	**23.** We often find the vowel phoneme in a closed syllable to be short. **A closed syllable ends with a consonant phoneme.** Study the words at the right. Underline the closed syllables, including closed one-syllable words. *chim ney* *men* *tree* *sun* *can* *win dow* *wish* *be gin*
short *don't, bird*	**24.** One vowel in a closed syllable (or in a one-syllable word) usually represents its _Short_ sound. With your key sentence in mind (frame 21), check the vowel phonemes in the following words. Which words do not have the short vowel phoneme? *clap* *don't* *skin* *sick* *trust* *fed* *bend* *bird*
yes *but ton* *pen cil* yes	**25.** Study the words at the right carefully. Is each syllable a closed syllable? _______ Write the closed syllables here: *but ton* *pen cil* Is there a single vowel in each syllable? _____________
unaccented	**26.** We might expect that we can properly indicate the pronunciation of each of the vowels with a breve. If you pronounce the words too carefully—that is, artificially—you might indicate their pronunciation that way. *but' ton* *pen' cil* Say a sentence aloud containing the word *button,* then one with *pencil.* You will notice that the vowel in the _____________ syllable (accented, unaccented) represents more of an "uh" sound and not the phonemes you hear in the words *ox* and *igloo.*

closed closed	**27.** Syllables with the CVC pattern are ______ (closed, open) syllables; those with the VC pattern (such as *ant*) are ______ (closed, open) syllables.
lĕm băn hŏp	**28.** The generalization for the short vowel phoneme is most useful when it is stated: **A single vowel in an accented closed syllable usually represents the short sound of the vowel.** Indicate the pronunciation of the syllables that follow this generalization: *re pay lem on ban jo hop per*
vowel short, *i*	**29.** We have noted the sounds represented by *a, e, i, o, u.* How about the *y?* Study the words at the right. Each contains a ______ (consonant, vowel) *y* within the syllable. The *y* represents the ______ (long, short) sound of the letter ____ . *gym* *sys tem* *sym bol*
fĭt (Any errors? Recheck the sound!) *păn* *stŏp* *pĕg*	**30.** Let us review the short sounds of the vowels. Check the words at the right against the key words you have learned. Place a breve above each of the vowels that represent the short sound of that vowel. *date put* *want fit* *pan stop* *peg cute*
short	**31.** We can expect that single vowels in closed accented syllables will usually represent ______ sounds. Remember that all one-syllable words are considered accented syllables.

shelve *pulse* *fence* short *rinse*	**32.** There are many words in which the vowel is followed by two consonants and a final *e*. Note that in words ending with a vowel that is followed by two consonants and a final *e*, the first vowel phoneme is usually _____________ . (short, long) Which words have the VCCe pattern?	*shelve* *pulse* *fence* *ride* *rinse* *smile*
e consonants short (unglided) silent	**33.** Study the words at the right. We can make a generalization concerning these words. When a word (or syllable) has two vowels, one of which is a final _____________ , and the two vowels are separated by two _____________ , the first vowel usually represents the _____________ sound and the final *e* is _____ .	*dance* *plunge* *dodge* *fence* *bronze* *lapse* *bridge* *smudge*
VCCe	**34.** The generalization is applied to words that have the ending pattern of VCCe (with exceptions, of course!). The word *lapse* is an example of VCCe pattern: vowel-consonant-consonant-final *e*. **When a word (or a syllable) has two vowels, one of which is a final *e*, and the two vowels are separated by two consonants, the final *e* is silent and the first vowel usually represents its short sound.** *Since* and *judge* end with the _____________ pattern.	
chance, ridge, since *sentence, prince*	**35.** Check the words below that end with the VCCe pattern. *chance* _____ *ridge* _____ *telephone* _____ *since* _____ *could* _____ *shape* _____ *tree* _____ *sentence* _____ *toy* _____ *prince* _____	
short	**36.** Study the words at the right. Note that in words ending with *-dge* the first vowel phoneme is usually _____________ . (short, long)	*bridge* *dodge* *smudge* *wedge*

BOX 3.1

Short Vowel Study Guide

Short Vowel	Key Symbol	Key Word
a	*ă*	*apple*
e	*ĕ*	*elephant*
i	*ĭ*	*igloo*
o	*ŏ*	*ox*
u	*ŭ*	*umbrella*

***Breve* (˘)** The breve (˘) is the diacritical mark used to indicate the specific pronunciation of the short vowels. *Unglided* is another term that refers to the short vowel phonemes.

CVC Pattern The most common vowel-consonant pattern is that of the CVC (consonant-vowel-consonant) in which the V (vowel) represents its short (unglided) sound (*pat, pet, pig, pot, puff*).

VC Pattern The V (vowel) in the VC pattern represents the short sound (*ant, etch, itch, odd, up*). The VC pattern functions the same as the CVC pattern.

VCCe Pattern When a word or a syllable has two vowels, one of which is a final *e,* and the two vowels are separated by two consonants, the first vowel usually represents the short sound and the final *e* is silent (*dance, fence, since, dodge, fudge*).

Closed Syllable A closed syllable ends with a consonant phoneme (*at*). A single vowel in an accented, closed syllable usually represents the short (unglided) sound of the vowel.

Ww as a Vowel As a vowel, the *w* represents no distinct phoneme of its own. The vowel *w* always follows another vowel in English words, and is used in combination with the other vowel (*new, cow, saw*).

Yy as a Vowel As a vowel, *y* represents no distinct phoneme of its own. When *y* is a vowel, its pronunciation is shown by the key symbols we associate with the *i* and the *e.* The vowel *y* is often silent (*play*).

	37. Now consider the following words.
	fence range paste hinge prance fudge
no	Is the VCCe pattern completely reliable? _____ (yes, no)

Answer	Frame
bed, pin	**38.** Now take time to study your own dictionary. Look up *bed.* Does the breve appear above the *e* in the pronunciation guide? Since the unglided vowel sound is so common, many dictionaries indicate the pronunciation of all short sounds with the letter alone (no diacritical mark). How would the pronunciation of *bed* be shown in these dictionaries? ____________ Of *pin?* ____________
ă ĕ ĭ ŏ ŭ *ăpple, ĕlephant, ĭgloo* *ŏx, ŭmbrella*	**39.** Write the key symbols we are using in this text to represent the short vowel phonemes. _____ _____ _____ _____ _____ Write the key words for each short vowel. Mark the vowel in each key word. Pronounce the short vowel phonemes. Can you say them rapidly? Practice them. Since they are so common, you should be familiar with them.

Review 14

1. Can you state the major generalization concerning short vowel sounds?
   a. Write the generalization that applies to the first two words at the right.
   b. State the generalization that applies to the vowel-consonant ending pattern in the last two words at the right.

   pet
   in
   since
   dance

2. We are studying the vowel phonemes that are represented by a single letter. We have learned to associate 5 of the 19 vowel phonemes with their key pronunciation symbols. Mark the vowels to indicate their pronunciations.

   bed next lot cat trip skin mop us send bug

3. Write the vowel-consonant pattern for the following words.

   up hat lapse tub ad rinse

4. We expect the single letter *g* to represent its hard sound, except when it is followed by _____ , _____ , or _____ .

   (See the Answers section for the answers to Review 14.)

Long Vowel Sounds

Answer	Frame
breves	*ā (apron)* *ē (eraser)* *ī (ice)* *ō (overalls)* *ū (unicorn)* **1.** This section introduces the long vowel sounds as shown above. Thus far we have identified five other vowel sounds. We call them "short" or unglided sounds. We distinguish the short vowels (as in the dictionary) from other vowel sounds by placing ____________ over them.
a ā apron *e ē eraser* *i ī ice* *o ō overalls* *u ū unicorn* name	*ā (apron)* *ē (eraser)* *ī (ice)* *ō (overalls)* *ū (unicorn)* **2.** One set of phonemes represented by single vowel letters is those which "say their own names." The key symbol for these vowel phonemes is a macron (-). Pronounce the first word at the right. Make the sound represented by the the underlined vowel; then say the name of the underlined vowel. 1 2 3 *a* *ā* *apron* ____ ____ *eraser* ____ ____ *ice* ____ ____ *overalls* ____ ____ *unicorn* The sound represented by the vowel is the same as the ____________ of the vowel. Pronounce the rest of the key words (3), vowel phonemes (key symbols) (2), and letter names (1) the same way. Complete the table. (Many dictionaries are now using an equivalent symbol, the *yōō,* to indicate the *ū.* Check your dictionary.)
ē, ī, ō, ū	**3.** We indicate the pronunciation of the vowel letter that "says its own name" by placing a **macron** (-) over it. Therefore the key symbol, as found in the dictionary, for the *a* in *apron* is *ā.* What would the key symbol be for each of the other underlined vowels in frame 2? ____ ____ ____ ____
pine	**4.** "Macron" contains the word element *macro,* which means "long" or "great." It has been the custom, in phonics, to call the vowel sound whose key symbol is a macron over the vowel letter a "long vowel sound." Therefore, we would say the *i* in ____________ represents a long (*pin, pine*) vowel sound.

long	**5.** It would seem that, in the normal pronunciation of words, we would hold long vowel sounds for a greater length of time than short vowel sounds. This is not necessarily true. Some texts now use the term "**glided sound**" rather than __________ (long, short) to indicate the sound of a vowel that "says its own name." We will use these terms interchangeably.
tāke, gō, fīne, bē, sāme (If you had any incorrect, study them carefully. Does the *a* in many "say its own name"?)	**6.** Place a macron above the vowels that represent long (glided) sounds in these words. Be sure the vowel "says its own name." *take go many fine once all be same*
no yo͞o is not o͞o	**7.** Though we will use the macron (*ū*), we will briefly consider the use of the *yo͞o* and the *o͞o* to indicate the long *ū*. Some teachers' manuals use the *yo͞o* to indicate the pronunciation of the long *ū* in *cube,* and the *o͞o* to indicate the pronunciation of the long *ū* in *tune.* Say *cube* and *tune.* Listen carefully. Do you hear different pronunciations of the long *u* in *cube* and *tune?* __________ (yes, no) A /*y*/ precedes the /*oo*/ in cube. This long vowel sound is therefore represented by ______ (*yo͞o, o͞o*). The sound that the *u* represents in *tune* __________ (is, is not) preceded by /*y*/. We would expect this sound to be represented by an __________ (*yo͞o, o͞o*). (Consult your teacher's manual for the symbols that are used to represent the long *ū*.)
cake, be, time *home, huge*	**8.** These five vowel phonemes are represented by the key symbols *ā, ē, ī, ō, ū*. Select a word from the list at the right which illustrates each. *ā* __________ *ē* __________ *ī* __________ *ō* __________ *ū* __________ *be up cake home huge time run*

nāmȩ, thēsȩ, cūtȩ, bōnȩ, toȩ, pīnȩ	**9.** Study the words below. Indicate those vowels that represent their long (glided) sounds by placing macrons above them. Put a diagonal line (/) through each vowel that is silent. *name these cute bone toe pine*
e, e long (glided)	**10.** There are many one-syllable words with two vowels in which *e* is the second vowel as well as the final letter of the word. We can make a generalization concerning these words. Study the words *name* and *pine;* then complete this generalization: When a one-syllable word has two vowels, one of which is a final _____ , the _____ is silent and the first vowel usually represents its _____________ sound.
VCe yes	**11.** This generalization most often applies to words that have the ending pattern of VCe. The word *use* is an example of VCe: vowel-consonant-final vowel *e.* *Time* and *plate* have the ending pattern of _____________ . Does this generalization apply to them? _____ . **When a one-syllable word has two vowels, one of which is the final *e,* the *e* is silent and the first vowel usually represents its long sound.**
VCe	**12.** The C in the consonant-vowel (VCe) pattern may signify a single consonant letter or a consonant digraph, but only one consonant phoneme. Since *ph* represents a single consonant phoneme, the nonsense word *sophe* has an ending pattern _____________ .
dīnȩ, hōpȩ, fācȩ, rīdȩ, cūbȩ, phōnȩ VCe	**13.** Mark each vowel in the following words with the proper diacritical mark. Put a slash (/) through the silent letters. *dine hope face ride cube phone* All of the above have the consonant-vowel ending pattern _____________ .

When a one-syllable word has two vowels, one of which is the final *e*, the *e* is silent and the first vowel usually represents its long sound.	**14.** Write the generalization concerning vowel sounds illustrated by the words: *ate game ice*
   come, some *there*	**15.** It is well to remember that the generalization is very helpful but not infallible. Check the words in the following set that do not follow the generalization. (Is the final *e* silent? Does the first vowel "say its own name"?) *come* _____ *place* _____ *these* _____ *some* _____ *there* _____ *late* _____ *clothe* _____ *same* _____
   dance *pāste* *fence* VCCe VCCe VCCe *wāste* *pulse* VCCe VCCe	**16.** This generalization is of little value in helping to determine the vowel sound in words ending with the consonant-vowel pattern of VCCe, even when such words are of one syllable. Study the words below. Indicate the vowels that represent the long sound by using the macron. *dance* *paste* *fence* *waste* *pulse* _____ _____ _____ _____ _____ Write the ending pattern (begin with the vowel) under each of the words.
  dăns, rīd, sāf, brĭj *kāk, fĕns* long (glided) short (unglided) silent	**17.** Write the words below to show pronunciation, using the key symbols we associate with each vowel and consonant letter. Omit each silent letter. *dance ride safe bridge cake fence* We can see that in one-syllable words which end with the pattern of VCe the first vowel is usually _____________ ; in one-syllable words which end with the pattern of VCCe the first vowel is usually _____________ . The final *e* in both patterns (VCe and VCCe) is usually _____________ .

lāte *pēde* VCe *rāde* *cāse* *tāke* *e, e* long	**18.** Mark the vowels in the last syllable in each of the words at the right to show pronunciation. The last syllable in each of these words has the vowel-consonant ending pattern of ____________ (VCe, VCCe). With these words in mind, our generalization might be extended to read: When a word or an accented syllable has two vowels, one of which is a final _____ , the _____ is silent and the first vowel usually represents its ____________ sound.	*re late* *stam pede* *pa rade* *book case* *mis take*
  v, l no arrive	**19.** All of the two- or more syllable words at the right have a final *e* which is silent. The consonant letter before the silent *e* in these words is either _____ or _____ . Does the last syllable in each of these words follow the generalization we have been studying? ____________ Underline the word(s) that does follow the generalization. Be sure you don't use an artificial pronunciation.	*active* *objective* *motive* *forgive* *legislative* *outlive* *arrive* *sterile* *automobile*
        ine	**20. When a word or an accented syllable has two vowels, one of which is a final *e*, the *e* is silent and the first vowel usually represents the long (glided) sound.** If we omit those words ending with *ve* and *le*, this generalization is of value in determining the vowel sounds in two- or more syllable words that have the ending pattern of VCe. **The *ve* and *le* endings are too irregular to be considered a reliable pattern.** Which of the following endings is most apt to follow the generalization at the beginning of this frame? *ale ive ave eve ine ole*	

	21. In frame 20, you identified ***ive*** and ***ave*** as too irregular to be of value in determining the vowel sounds of words that have the ending pattern of **VCe.** Rewrite the words below, omitting the final ***e:***
	love *prove* *have* *give* *glove*
lov, prov, hav, giv, glov	_____ _____ _____ _____ _____
	Puzzle: Why do these words end in a final ***e*** if the **VCe** pattern does not help us determine the pronunciation of the vowel sound?
	Hint: Look at the words that you have rewritten. Do they look like
No	English words? ____________
	The final ***e*** follows the letter ***v*** in words such as *love, have,* and *give* because English words do not end in the letter ***v.***
Follow: *stove, cone, throne, globe* Do Not Follow: *come, one, none, some*	**22.** Let us consider another exception. Say the words at the right. Listen carefully to the sound that the vowel *o* represents. Arrange the words in two columns: (1) those in which the ending pattern **VCe** is of value in determining the pronunciation of the vowel, and (2) those in which the ending pattern **VCe** does not help us determine the pronunciation of the vowel. *stove cone come one throne none globe some* Words do not follow the generalization when the vowel letter *o* is pronounced like the sound of "uh" in the word *done.*
	23. We have identified five vowel phonemes that represent the
long (or glided)	____________ sounds of the letters.
(All words below must have a silent, final *e.*)	We have also learned one generalization which gives a clue to that sound. Select one word for each of the five vowels to illustrate this generalization. Place a macron above the vowels selected.
rōle, remāke, extrēme	*shady* *one* *role* *piece* *remake*
prīce, cūbe	*extreme* *come* *price* *cube* *dance*
	24. We have noted that when we see a word or an accented syllable with the pattern of a single vowel followed by a single
consonant	____________ and final *e,* the single vowel is likely to represent its
long (glided)	____________ sound. The vowel-consonant ending pattern we
VCe	expect to see is ____________ .

BOX 3.2

Final *E* Solves Four Tricky Spelling Problems

Before spelling was finalized in the seventeenth century, early writers used the final *e* to solve several tricky spelling problems. We will consider four ways in which the final *e* came to the rescue.

1. English words ending with a /v/ or a /z/ phoneme presented a sticky spelling problem for early writers. Although English words can end with a /v/ or /z/ phoneme (*groove, breeze*), spelling conventions did not provide for a single *v* or *z* to be the final letter (*groov, breez*). The inventive writers added a final *e* to avoid ending words with a final *v* or *z* grapheme (e.g., *starve, swerve, bronze, snooze*).
2. Early writers needed a way to indicate when the *th* is voiced (*teethe*) and when it is unvoiced (*teeth*). In solving their problem, the inventive writers once again used the final *e,* adding it to words such as *teethe* and *clothe* so as to avoid confusion with words such as *teeth* and *cloth.*
3. The final *e* also came in handy when spelling words that end in /*s*/. Sometimes the /*s*/ is part of the root word (*dense*); sometimes it is part of a suffix (*dens*). In using the final *e,* the writers of yesteryear generously provided the reader with a helpful visual cue for sorting out when the letter *s* is part of a root word (*tens + e = tense, brows + e = browse*) and when the final *s* is part of a suffix (*horse + s = horses; lapse + s = lapses*).
4. Thanks to the final *e,* it is clear when to use the soft *c (key word: sun)* and *g (key word: jeep)* in words such as *choice* and *damage.* Without the final *e,* the reader might be tempted to pronounce *choic* (choice) as /choik/ and *damag* (damage) as /damag/.

English is a dynamic and evolving language in which spelling changes occur over relatively long periods of time. Will the final *e* eventually drop away from words in which the *e* neither contributes to pronunciation nor gives the reader an important visual clue? No one knows—but we might speculate. Generally speaking, American spelling changes make words simpler, such as dropping the *u* from the British *colour* or the trendy *nite* for *night.* So perhaps the writers in some future century will spell *groove* and *breeze* as *groov* and *breez.*

	pīne	*cūte*	**25.** All the vowels at the right represent the	*pin*	*cut*
short	*rāte*	*strīpe*	____________ sounds. Check each one to make sure.	*rat*	*strip*
	kīte	*pāle*		*kit*	*pal*
	hāte	*āte*	Now attach a silent *e* at the end of each word to see what happens. To show the new pronunciation, mark the first vowel in each of the new words you've made with the appropriate diacritical mark.	*hat*	*at*
long			The vowels now represent their ____________ sounds.		

e pronunciation (or sound)	**26.** We can see that the silent _____ at the end of a word has a purpose. It changes the meaning of the word as well as the ______________ of the word.	*cut* *cute* *strip* *stripe*
so *so lo* *fe ver* *ti ger* *me* *pa per*	**27.** Another situation in which we often find the vowel to be long is that of the open syllable. **An open syllable ends with a vowel phoneme.** Study the words at the right. Underline the open syllables, including open one-syllable words.	*so* *sup pose* *so lo* *fe ver* *pine* *ti ger* *me* *pa per*
    CV open	**28.** This generalization most often applies to words and syllables that have the vowel-consonant pattern of CV. Study the words and the underlined syllables below. *me* *be long* *ma ple* *so* The words and the underlined syllables have the vowel-consonant pattern of _____ . Each of the above words and underlined syllables is a(n) ______________ syllable. (open, closed)	
consonant phoneme silent	**29.** The first syllable of *sup pose* ends with a ______________ phoneme. The second syllable of *sup pose* is not an open syllable because it does not end with a vowel ______________ . The last letter is a vowel, but it (letter, phoneme) is ______________ .	
yes *ē* *CV, no* *r*	**30.** Is the first syllable of *fe ver* an open syllable? ______________ What key symbol represents the final phoneme of the first syllable? _____ The first syllable in *fe ver* has the consonant-vowel pattern of _____ . Is the second syllable an open syllable? _______ What key symbol represents the final phoneme? _____	

long	**31.** Study these words: *hel lo* *be* *me ter* *ti ger* The underlined vowels represent their ____________ sounds. (long, short)	
fā *hē* open *sī* glided (or long) *tō* CV *hū*	**32.** Place a macron above the five vowels (*a, e, i, o, u*) that represent their glided sounds in the words at the right. We might generalize: A single vowel in an _____ syllable often represents its ____________ sound. The vowel-consonant pattern for an open syllable is _____ .	*fa vor* *he* *si lent* *to tal* *hu man*
sō lō *bē long* *dī graph* *hā lō* *hel lō* *do*	**33.** Study the words at the right. Draw a line under the single vowels in the open syllables. Place a macron above those vowels you underlined which represent the long sound. Work carefully. You may find exceptions.	*so lo* *be long* *di graph* *ha lo* *hel lo* *do*
e open	**34.** Although the *a* in *about* and the _____ in *debate* are single vowel letters in ____________ syllables, they do (closed, open) not represent long sounds. **We tend to shorten the vowel sounds in unaccented syllables.**	*a bout* *de bate*
long (glided)	**35.** The generalization has more application when we limit it to accented syllables: A single vowel in an open accented syllable usually represents its ____________ sound. We will study this more fully later.	

Answers	Frame	Words
lō, lō	**36.** We should note, however, that sometimes single vowel letters in open unaccented syllables do represent the long sounds. Two syllables from the words at the right which illustrate this are _____ from *solo* and _____ from *halo.* Mark the vowels in these unaccented syllables.	*so′ lo* *ha′ lo*
pa pa to	**37.** We should also note that not all vowels in open accented syllables represent long sounds. (Exceptions, exceptions!) Underline the syllables that are exceptions to the generalization: **Single vowel letters in open accented syllables usually represent their long sounds.**	*no* *pa′pa* *to* *she*
short no long silent	**38.** We will now consider long vowel exceptions to the closed syllable generalization. We expect that single vowels in closed syllables—the CVC and VC patterns—will usually represent _____________ sounds. (long, short) Do the words at the right follow the closed syllable generalization? _____ **An exception to the generalization is found in words in which the *i* is followed by *gh*.** The *i* represents the _____________ sound and the *gh* is _____________ in such words. (long, short)	*sight* *high* *right* *sight* *sigh*
ld	**39.** The words below represent another exception to the closed syllable generalization. *child wild mild sold told hold* We can summarize: **When *i* or *o* is followed by _____ , the vowel usually represents the long sound.**	

closed closed open phoneme	**40.** Let us review. Syllables with the CVC pattern are ________ (closed, open) syllables; those with the VC pattern (such as *ant*) are ________ (closed, open) syllables. Syllables that have the CV pattern are ________ (closed, open) syllables. An open syllable ends with a vowel ________ (phoneme, letter).
a, e, i, o, u	**41.** The previous frames in this section contain examples of the five vowels, _____, _____, _____, _____, and _____, in which they represent their long sounds.
vowel	**42.** We have learned that the vowel *w* always appears with another ________ letter. Therefore, there would be no instances in which we could apply the single-vowel open syllable generalization to the *w*.
bī *mī* *whī* *flī* ī *krī* CV	**43.** Let us examine the generalization with respect to the vowel *y*. Look at the words at the right. In each instance the *y* represents the phoneme we associate with the key symbol _____. The vowel-consonant pattern for these words is _____. Rewrite these words. Use the key symbol we associate with each vowel and consonant phoneme. *by* ________ *my* ________ *why* ________ *fly* ________ *cry* ________
long *e*	**44.** Study the words at the right. Complete the generalization: When *y* is the final letter of a two-syllable word, it represents the ________ sound of _____. *happy* *lucky* *baby* *windy*

bī pas *sī pres* *pī thon*	**45.** *Y* is not always the final letter in a word. Study the words at the right. Rewrite them to show the pronunciation of the consonants and of the vowels representing the long sounds.	*by pass* __________ *cy press* __________ *py thon* __________
cry *lucky*	**46.** If *y* represents the long sound of the *e* when it is the final and only vowel in the last syllable of a multisyllabic word, then the open syllable generalization we have been studying applies to *a, e, i, o, u,* and *y.* The *y* would represent the sound of the long *i* in __________ (*cry, happy*) and the long *e* in __________ (*my, lucky*).	
A single vowel in an open accented syllable often represents its long sound.	**47.** State the generalization that concerns a single vowel in an open accented syllable.	

BOX 3.3

The Extra *E*

Exception words such as *gone* and *done,* which we expect to be pronounced with a long *e,* are a consequence of the quirky way in which the English spelling system developed. Before the fourteenth century, the final *e* represented an "uh" which was pronounced at the end of words. To get a sense of how contemporary words would sound with a final "uh," say *gone* and *done,* and then add an extra "uh" to the end—"gonuh" and "donuh." Sometime around the fourteenth century the "uh" was dropped from pronunciation, and the final *e* became the silent letter in words spelled with the VCe pattern.

Then something curious happened. For some unknown reason, the early writers began to attach a final *e* to short vowel words which ended in a consonant letter. The writers usually doubled the final consonant, suggesting that they knew that the final *e* in the VCe pattern signaled that the preceding vowel is long. Put into a contemporary context, the word *pit* might be spelled *pitte,* and *pin* as *pinne.* For some time, English spelling was cluttered with extra consonants and final ***e*** s. Spelling was eventually untangled in the seventeenth century when the practice of adding an extra *e* to the end of short vowel words was discontinued. However, some of the words from this earlier period still continue to be spelled with the unnecessary final *e,* which is the reason why we have words such as *gone* and *done* in our English language dictionary today.

BOX 3.4

Long Vowel Study Guide

Long Vowel	Key Symbol	Key Word
a	*ā*	*apron*
e	*ē*	*eraser*
i	*ī*	*ice*
o	*ō*	*overalls*
u	*ū*	*unicorn*

Macron (-) The macron (-) is the diacritical mark used to indicate the specific pronunciation of the long vowels. *Glided* is another term that refers to the long vowel phonemes.

Long ū Some dictionaries are now using the *(y)o͞o* to indicate the *ū*. Some teachers' manuals use two symbols to indicate the *ū*—the *yo͞o* for the *ū* in *unicorn* and *cube,* and o͞o for the *ū* in *tune* and *true.*

VCe Pattern When a word or an accented syllable has two vowels, one of which is a final *e,* the *e* is silent and the first vowel usually represents the long (glided) sound (*ape, hope*).

le and ve Exceptions to the VCe Pattern The *le* or *ve* endings are too irregular to be considered reliable representations of the VCe pattern (*have, love*).

o Pronounced as "uh" *Exception to the VCe Pattern* Words do not follow the VCe generalization when the vowel letter *o* is pronounced like the "uh" in the words *done* and *come.*

Open Syllable An open syllable ends with a vowel phoneme (*be, try*). Single vowel letters in open, accented syllables usually represent their long (glided) sounds (*she*).

Unaccented Syllables We tend to shorten vowel sounds in unaccented syllables (*a bout'*).

CV Pattern The CV pattern is an open syllable in which the vowel usually represents its long sound (*be, tree*).

Yy as a Vowel When *y* is the final letter in a one-syllable word (*my*), it usually represents the sound we associate with long *i* (key word: *ice*). When *y* is the final letter in a two-syllable word (*happy*), it usually represents the long sound of *e* (key word: *eraser*).

igh Exception When the *i* is followed by *gh* in a word or a syllable, the *i* usually represents the long sound and the *gh* is silent (*light*).

i or o Followed by ld When *i* or *o* is followed by *ld,* the vowel usually represents the long sound (*wild, fold*).

Review 15

1. We have been studying five phonemes which represent the long sounds of the vowels: *ā*, _____ , _____ , _____ , _____ . We can show their pronunciation by placing a _____________ (name of diacritical mark) over each of them.
2. *Y* can represent a long sound also, but it does not have a key symbol: It is a duplication of either the long _____ (as in *cry*) or the long _____ (as in *lucky*).
3. We have learned to recognize two patterns which may give clues as to the vowel sound in an unknown word. One is the vowel-consonant-silent _____ pattern (VCe). State the generalization:
4. The other is a single-vowel, open syllable pattern: The single vowel in an open, _____________ syllable is often_____________ .
5. Another way we can state the same generalization is: When the only vowel in a word or accented syllable comes at the_____________ of the syllable, that vowel usually represents its _____________ sound.
6. The long sounds of the vowels are easiest to recognize in known words because the name of the vowel is the same as the _____________ it represents.
7. Pronounce the words at the right.
   a. Place a C behind each word that ends with a consonant phoneme.
   b. Place a V behind each word that ends with a vowel phoneme.
   c. Indicate the pronunciation of the final phoneme by writing the key symbol. If the word ends with a consonant blend, use only the symbol which represents the final phoneme in the blend.
   d. Underline the words in which the final syllable is an open syllable.

dine	*table*
tack	*hello*
way	*tight*
watch	*enough*

8. We are studying the vowel phonemes that are represented by a single letter. We have learned to associate 10 of the 19 vowel phonemes with their key pronunciation symbols. Mark the following vowel graphemes to indicate their pronunciation.

   bite bit can cane pet Pete us fuse cot code

(See the Answers section for the answers to Review 15.)

Schwa (ə)

a ə *comma* *e* ə *chicken* *i* ə *family* *o* ə *button* *u* ə *circus*	(*comma, chicken, family, button, circus*) **1.** Say the words at the right aloud. Listen to the phoneme represented by the underlined letter. When you say the words slowly and distinctly (and artificially), they may sound quite different from one another; but when these words are used in ordinary speech, the underlined part represents a very soft "uh." The letters that represent the "uh" sound in the words at the right are ____, ____, ____, ____, ____. Place them properly in column 1.
ə	**2.** Dictionaries usually indicate the soft vowel sound found in unaccented syllables with a **schwa (ə).** The pronunciation is shown by the sign ____ (an inverted *e*).
blend	**3.** How is the *schwa* pronounced? The *sch* grapheme in *schwa* represents the phoneme we associate with the key symbol *sh.* The *sh* and the consonant *w* form a ________ (digraph, blend). The *a* represents an "ah" sound.
commə *chickən* *faməly* *buttən* *circəs*	**4.** Rewrite the words at the right to show the pronunciation of the vowel in the unaccented syllable. Without the schwa, each of these vowels would need a separate diacritical mark.
bā′ kən	**5.** **The schwa is used to indicate the pronunciation of the vowel phoneme in many unaccented syllables.** Study the word below. Rewrite it, indicating the sound of each letter. *ba′ con* ______

Frame 1 word list:

1	2	3
____	ə	*comma*
____	ə	*chicken*
____	ə	*family*
____	ə	*button*
____	ə	*circus*

Frame 4 word list:

com′ ma	____
chick′ en	____
fam′ i ly	____
but′ ton	____
cir′ cus	____

pĕns əl *li ən* *sĕk ənd* *prŏb ləm* *a, e, i, o, u*	**6.** Say the words at the right in a natural manner. Rewrite them, using key symbols to indicate each of the phonemes. *pencil* _____ *lion* _____ *second* _____ *problem* _____ Check the vowels that can represent the schwa phoneme: *a* _____ *e* _____ *i* _____ *o* _____ *u* _____
unaccented	**7.** The use of the schwa for each vowel that represents the short "uh" sound, along with the frequent use of the short *i* (i), has simplified pronunciation keys greatly. Almost all vowels in ______________ syllables represent one of these (accented, unaccented) two short, soft sounds.
ə *i*	**8.** Let us examine the words *distant* and *village.* The dictionary may indicate the pronunciation as dĭs′ tənt and vĭl′ ĭj. The _____ and the _____ indicate the two soft phonemes regardless of spelling.
facet, sicken *banquet, melon*	**9.** The following words are written to show their pronunciation. What are the words? *făs′ ĭt* _____ *sĭk′ ən* _____ *băng′ kwĭt* _____ *mĕl′ ən* _____
vegetable, possible	**10.** Examine the words below. They are written the way they might appear in your dictionary. What are the words? *vĕj′ tə bəl* ______________ *pŏs′ ə bəl* ______________ Note that we pronounce the syllable *ble* as though a very short vowel precedes the *l: bəl.*
er, tig ər	**11.** Although the word part *er* has only a touch of a vowel sound, the schwa is used with the *r* to indicate the pronunciation of the word part _____ . Thus the key symbols for *tiger* are ______________ . (Check your dictionary to see how it treats this word part.)

stā′ bəl, mī′ nəs bŏt′ əm, dĭf′ ər	**12.** Rewrite the words below to show pronunciation. Omit the silent letters. *sta′ ble* _____ *mi′ nus* _____ *bot′ tom* _____ *dif′ fer* _____
sō′ fə, plĕzh′ ər kwĭv′ ər, drān′ ĭj kō′ kō, bī′ sĭk əl	**13.** Are you ready to code some more difficult words? Rewrite the words below to show pronunciation. They should be written as they might appear in parentheses following the boldface entry word in the dictionary. To avoid artificial pronunciation, check each one by saying it in a sentence. *so′ fa* _____ *pleas′ ure* _____ *quiv′ er* _____ *drain′ age* _____ *co′ coa* _____ *bi′ cy cle* _____
sĭm′ fə nē (or nĭ) ĭ mŭl′ shən dĭf′ ə kŭlt, ăn tēk′	**14.** Rewrite the words below to show pronunciation. They should be written as they might appear in parentheses following the boldface entry word in the dictionary. To avoid artificial pronunciation, check each one by saying it in a sentence. *sym′ pho ny* _____________ *e mul′ sion* _____________ *dif′ fi cult* _____________ *an tique′* _____________
short *i*	**15.** The first vowel in *decay* represents the __________ phoneme. This use represents the trend toward simplification. It is not *e.* Try it in a sentence to check this. Now try it using *i* as a guide in pronouncing the first syllable.
hăp′ ən (or *hap′ ən*)	**16.** It is necessary to note that various dictionaries indicate pronunciation in different ways. We must study the pronunciation key of the particular dictionary we use. For example, many dictionaries indicate the pronunciation of all short sounds with the letter and no diacritical mark. The pronunciation of *happen* is written _____________ .
village *pilot*	**17.** Let us review. We have learned that a vowel grapheme in an unaccented syllable could reasonably be expected to represent the sound we associate with the unglided *i* (short *i*) or with the sound represented by the schwa (ə). The *i* would identify the vowel phonemes in the last syllable of _____________ . The ə would (*candy, program, village, hotel*) identify the last syllable of _____________ . (*pilot, locate, liquid, railroad*)

BOX 3.5

Schwa Study Guide

Vowel in an Unaccented Syllable	Key Symbol	Key Word
a	ə	*comma* (soft "uh")
e	ə	*chicken* (soft "uh")
i	ə	*family* (soft "uh")
o	ə	*button* (soft "uh")
u	ə	*circus* (soft "uh")

Vowels in Unaccented Syllables The vowels in unaccented syllables can reasonably be expected to represent a soft "uh," or the sound we associate with an unglided (short) *ĭ*.

Schwa The dictionary uses a schwa (ə) to indicate the soft "uh" sound found in many unaccented syllables. Without the schwa (ə), the vowels that represent the soft "uh" in unaccented syllables would each need a separate diacritical mark to indicate pronunciation.

Short ĭ The vowels in unaccented syllables may also represent the unglided (short) *ĭ*, such as in *manage* (*măn′ ĭj*). The vowels in unaccented syllables represent the soft "uh," the schwa, more often than the short *ĭ*.

Review 16

1. The key symbol used to represent many of the vowel phonemes in unaccented syllables is called a ______________ (ə).
2. This symbol is very useful because ______________ .
3. The ə*r* is used to indicate the pronunciation of a word part in ______________ .
   (*river, erase*)
4. The words below are written to show their pronunciation. How are they correctly spelled?

   rē′ gəl   *hănd mād′*   *sĕl′ ə brāt*   *ĕp′ ə sōd*

   (See the Answers section for the answers to Review 16.)

Other Single Vowels

five, schwa phoneme	**1.** Thus far we have identified 11 vowel phonemes using only ______ vowel letters and a _____ . (How many?) We can readily tell which ______ is represented when (letter, phoneme) diacritical marks are used, as in a dictionary, glossary, or other pronunciation guide.
short (unglided)	**2.** We also have examined patterns common to the English language so that we can make a reasonable guess as to the sound of certain vowels. For example, we expect the vowel letter in the pattern CVC to represent its ______ sound.
apple	**3.** If the vowel in the CVC pattern is *a,* then we would expect *a* to represent the same sound as the vowel phoneme heard in ______ . (*said, car, ball, apple, date, saw*)
glided (long) silent	**4.** We expect the first vowel grapheme in the ending pattern VCe to represent its ______ sound and the final *e* to be ______ .
sew	**5.** If the first vowel grapheme in the VCe ending pattern is an *o,* then we would expect *o* to represent the same vowel phoneme as that heard in ______ . (*done, gone, boy, sew*)
schwa *sofa*	**6.** A vowel in an unaccented syllable could reasonably be expected to represent the sound we associate with the unglided (short) *i* or with the ______ . The ə would identify the vowel phoneme in the last syllable of ______ . (*sofa, remit, require, insect*)

Answers	Frame
a *â* *care* *u* *û* *fur* *a* *ä* *father* *a* *ô* *ball* graphemes	**7.** There are still other single vowel phonemes as shown at the right. Some are influenced by the consonant following the vowel. We will identify these vowel phonemes and suggest a key word by which each can be remembered. However, we commonly use the pronunciation key given at the bottom of the page in the dictionary for these more difficult phonemes. Each of these phonemes is represented by a variety of spellings, in other words, by a variety of ____________ . (sounds, graphemes) 1 | 2 | 3 *a* | _____ | *câre (kâr)* *u* | _____ | *fûr* *a* | _____ | *fäther (fäthər)* *a* | _____ | *ball (bôl)* Complete the table by filling in the key symbols (2). We have noted that various dictionaries use different ways to indicate pronunciation. Check the pronunciation key in your dictionary for the key symbols for these four vowel phonemes.
r	**8.** Let's examine the vowel phoneme in the key word *care.* The key symbol we will use to represent this phoneme is *â.* We can hardly separate it from the following consonant phoneme, so we call it _____-controlled. (*r, l, w*)
yes six	**9.** Study the words at the right. Pronounce each word aloud. Is the vowel phoneme the same in each word? ____________ . In these examples, one vowel phoneme is represented by _____ graphemes. (How many?) *chair* *share* *their* *there* *bear* *prayer*
ai, a, ei, e, ea, ay	**10.** Underline the graphemes that represent the same vowel phoneme heard in *care.* They represent vowel phonemes, so do not underline the controlling consonant. *chair* *share* *their* *there* *bear* *prayer* You can see that our table, frame 7, is greatly oversimplified. Column 1 should show the six graphemes that, when followed by *r,* represent the vowel phoneme we hear in *care.*

	11. Rewrite the words below, using the key symbols to indicate the pronunciation of consonants and vowels. Omit silent letters.
kâr, whâr, fârē	care __________ *where* __________ *fairy* __________
shâr, hâr, băt	*share* __________ *hair* __________ *bat* __________
bat	The word out of place in this list is __________ .
	12. The following words are written as they would appear in a dictionary to show pronunciation. Spell them correctly.
air, anchor, square	*âr* __________ *ăngʹ kər* __________ *skwâr* __________
pile, scarce, chair	*pīl* __________ *skârs* __________ *châr* __________
race, civic, their	*rās* __________ *sĭvʹ ĭk* __________ *t̸hâr* __________
or *there*	You can interpret the dictionary code!
i	**13.** Another vowel phoneme which is *r*-controlled is the one heard in *fur.* In fact, it is impossible to separate it from the _____ . *thirst*
e	*germ*
r *ea*	*learn*
o	Say the words at the right. What graphemes represent the vowel phoneme heard in *fur* as shown by the words at the right? Underline them. *worm*
u	*purple*
y	*myrtle*
	14. Rewrite the words above using the *û* to show the pronunciation of that part of the word.
thûrst, jûrm, lûrn	__________ __________ __________
wûrm, pûrpəl, mûrtəl	__________ __________ __________
	15. Note that this phoneme is not the same as that heard as a separate syllable, generally a suffix, as in *farmer, lower.* We will identify this separate syllable by *ər.* Rewrite the following words to show pronunciation:
wûrkər, wûrkt, snâr	*worker* __________ *worked* __________ *snare* __________

sûrv *pāpər* *skûrt* *hâr*	**16.** Rewrite the words at the right to show their pronunciation. *serve* ____________ *paper* ____________ *skirt* ____________ *hair* ____________
several different *fur*	**17.** The phoneme that we associate with the key symbol *û* may be represented by ____________ graphemes. The key word chosen to (only one, several different) help us remember this phoneme is ____________ .
several different *care*	**18.** The phoneme that we associate with the key symbol *â* may be represented by ____________ graphemes. Its key word is (only one, several different) ________________ .
graphemes (or spellings)	**19.** The phoneme that we will identify with the key symbol *ä* and the key word *father* may be confusing because of regional differences in pronunciation. It is represented by many different letters and combinations of letters. Dictionaries reveal anywhere from 3 to 11 different ____________ which represent this phoneme.
ä	**20.** Pronounce the words at the right. If you do not hear the vowel phoneme you hear in *father,* your pronunciation is simply reflecting a regional difference. You are not wrong. Now pronounce them so that you can hear the phoneme we represent by the key symbol _____ in each one. *arm* *calm* *hearth* *sergeant* *bazaar*
a, al, ea, e, aa	**21.** In the words below, underline the graphemes that represent the phoneme we identify by *ä.* Include the silent letters that could be considered a part of the grapheme. *arm* *calm* *hearth* *sergeant* *bazaar*

Answers	Frames
fär, täcō, pläzə *cäm, gärd, dâr*	**22.** If you cannot agree with the pronunciation, use your dictionary. Your pronunciation may reflect that of your region. Use the key symbols to show the pronunciation of these words: *far* ______ *taco* ______ *plaza* ______ *calm* ______ *guard* ______ *dare* ______
kärnāshən, bärnyärd, bâr *pârənt, kāk, hûrt*	**23.** Rewrite these words to show pronunciation: *carnation* ______ *barnyard* ______ *bear* ______ *parent* ______ *cake* ______ *hurt* ______
raw, caught, walk, broad *fought, tall, order*	**24.** Pronounce *ball.* Listen to the vowel phoneme. We will represent this phoneme with the key symbol *ô.* Say the words below. Check those in which you hear the phoneme heard in *ball.* *raw* ____ *caught* ____ *walk* ____ *broad* ____ *bead* ____ *fought* ____ *tall* ____ *order* ____ Some of the answers here may also be affected by regional variations in pronunciation. Check your dictionary. Do you have trouble with the word *order?* Would you believe that many dictionaries use *order, for,* and *horn* as the key words?
aw, au, al, oa, ou, a, o	**25.** What graphemes in frame 24 represent the vowel phoneme heard in *ball?* ____ ____ ____ ____ ____ ____ ____
rô, kôt, wôk, brôd *bēd, fôt, tôl, ôrder*	**26.** Rewrite the words in frame 24 using key symbols to indicate pronunciation. ______ ______ ______ ______ ______ ______ ______ ______
ball sô	**27.** Pronounce *saw.* The *a* represents the vowel phoneme in ______ . (*ball, sat*) When *a* is followed by an *l* or *w* in the same syllable, the *a* may represent the sound we associate with the key symbol *ô.* Rewrite *saw* to show pronunciation. ______

 shawl, small false, drawn	**28.** These words are written to show their pronunciation. What are the words? *shôl* ______ *smôl* ______ *fôls* ______ *drôn* ______
    3, 1, 3, 2, 4 1, 3, 4, 4	**29.** Let us review: Four single-vowel phonemes are represented by the underlined letters at the right. 1. *â* *care* 2. *ä* *father* 3. *ô* *ball* 4. *û* *fur* Indicate the pronunciation of the underlined vowels in the words below by using the number of the word in which the vowel has the same pronunciation. *fault* ____ *repair* ____ *Utah* ____ *sergeant* ____ *term* ____ *there* ____ *broad* ____ *courage* ____ *work* ____
    short *r*	**30.** There are a few broad generalizations which may be of some help in determining the pronunciation of these vowels in unknown words. **If the only vowel letter in a word or syllable is followed by *r*, the vowel will be affected by that *r*.** Say the words at the right. The vowel sounds are neither long nor ______ . They are almost lost in the consonant letter ____ . *car* *farmer* *curl* *first* *corn*
  late no *yes*	**31. If the only vowel in a word or syllable is an *a* followed by *l* or *w*, the *a* is affected by that *l* or *w*.** Study the words at the right. Which word does not belong in the list? ______ Do any of the others represent the long or short sound of *a?* ______ Does the *a* followed by *l* represent the same sound as the *a* followed by *w?* ______ Again, regional variations in the pronunciation of these words may cause you some difficulty. *draw* *saw* *late* *fall* *small*

BOX 3.6

Other Single Vowels Study Guide

Vowel Letter	Key Symbol	Key Word
a	*â*	*care*
u	*û*	*fur*
a	*ä*	*father*
a	*ô*	*ball*

R-Controlled Vowels When the only vowel letter in a word or syllable is followed by *r,* the vowel will be affected by that *r.* When pronouncing a vowel followed by the *r,* the vowel phoneme is almost lost in the consonant.

R-Controlled â(r) It is impossible to separate, in normal pronunciation, the /*â*/ from the /*r*/. Six graphemes represent the *â* when followed by *r: care, hair, heir, wear, where,* and *prayer.*

R-Controlled û(r) It is impossible to separate, in normal pronunciation, the /*û*/ from the /*r*/. Several graphemes represent the *û*(*r*), as we see in the words *first, germ, learn, worm, purple,* and *myrtle.*

R-Controlled ä(r) The *a,* when preceding the letter *r,* represents an *r*-controlled vowel. Examples of the *r*-controlled *a,* pronounced as /*är*/, may be heard in the words *arm, yard, arch,* and *large.* This phoneme may also be spelled with the *ea* grapheme, as in *hearth,* and the *er,* as in *sergeant.*

R-Controlled ô(r) The *o,* when preceding the letter *r,* represents an *r*-controlled vowel. Examples of the *r*-controlled *o,* pronounced as /*ôr*/, may be heard in the words *more, court,* and *order.*

ä The *ä,* key word *father,* does not always precede the letter *r* in English words. Several graphemes represent the *ä,* as shown in the words *calm, cot, shah,* and *bazaar.*

ô The *ô,* key word *ball,* is heard in *caught* and *broad.* Several graphemes represent the *ô,* as shown in the words *saw, caught, walk, broad,* and *fought.*

a Before l or w (ô) When the letter *a* is the only vowel in a word or syllable, and precedes the letter *l* or the letter *w,* the *a* is affected by the *l* or *w,* and is pronounced /*ô*/. Notice the difference in the phonemes in which the letter *a* represents in *bald* (*bôld*) and *bad* (*băd*), and in *jaw* (*jô*) and *jam* (*jăm*). Examples include *call, almost, talk, draw, awful,* and *shawl.*

Review 17

1. We have been studying the vowel phonemes that can be represented by single-vowel key symbols. The first group of five (example, *apple*) we labeled

   the ______________ vowel phonemes. Write their key symbols:

2. The second group of five (example, *ice*) we labeled ______________ vowel phonemes. Write their key symbols:

3. The third (example, *comma*) was given a key symbol not in the alphabet, called the ______________ . This key symbol, ______, represents each of the vowels when they have the sound heard in ______________ . It is very useful
(*happy, agree*)
because ______________ .

4. That left us with four additional single-vowel phonemes which cannot be grouped except for the influence on them of the phoneme ________________
(following, preceding)
the vowel. We found that they were affected by phonemes represented by the _____ , _____ , and _____ .

5. The key words for these vowel phonemes can be placed in the following sentences. Fill in the blanks and mark the vowels.

   a. She hit the ______________ over the fence.

   b. The kitten has soft, fluffy _____ .

   c. Tom's _____ will take Tom on a fishing trip next Saturday.

   d. The mother dog takes good _____ of her puppies.

   (See the Answers section for the answers to Review 17.)

Diphthongs

consonant *l*	*oi (oil)* *ou (house)* 1. We have been studying the vowel phonemes that are represented by single vowel letters. We will now turn our attention to those which are represented by combinations of letters. Say *oil.* The word *oil* is composed of two phonemes: one vowel and one ______________ . They are represented by the graphemes *oi* and _____ .
diphthongs (Check the spelling.)	2. The *oi* functions as one phoneme called a **diphthong.** **A diphthong is a single vowel phoneme, represented by two letters, resembling a glide from one sound to another.** A study of **phonetics** (the science of speech sounds) would show that many single-letter vowels are actually diphthongs. They represent more than a single sound. Note the gliding sound of the *u* in *use.* You may be using "glided" rather than "long" for this vowel phoneme. We will call only the two-letter gliding combinations ______________ .

Answer	Frame
diphthong	**3.** In this study we have made the arbitrary statement that there are 44 phonemes. It really is not that simple! Say *few.* Is the vowel phoneme equivalent to the phoneme heard at the beginning of *use,* or should we consider *ew* a separate diphthong, not a duplication of any single vowel phoneme? Our decision is to consider that *few* = *fū.* So we will not call *ew* a ___________ .
oi, ou	**4.** It seems most helpful to classify only two of the vowel phonemes as diphthongs. These are the vowel sounds heard in *oil* and *house.* The _____ and the _____ then represent 2 of the 44 speech sounds in our language.
oi oy — *boil, boy, coin, enjoy, toy*	**5.** Examine the words at the right. Underline the grapheme in each word that represents the diphthong *oi.* There are two spellings which represent this diphthong: _____ and _____ . *boil* *boy* *coin* *enjoy* *toy*
boil, boi, koin, ĕnjoi, toi *oi*	**6.** Rewrite the five words above using the marks of pronunciation (the diacritical marks). _____ _____ _____ _____ _____ The key word for this diphthong is *oil,* the key symbol _____ .
house, brown, cow, mouse, blouse, owl — *ou, ow*	**7.** The second diphthong is that heard in the key word *house.* The key symbol is *ou.* Read the words at the right. Underline the diphthongs. This diphthong is also represented by two spellings: the _____ and the _____ *house* *brown* *cow* *mouse* *blouse* *owl*
1 / 2 / 3 *oi, oy* / *oi* / *oil* *ou, ow* / *ou* / *house*	**8.** Complete the table at the right with the two spellings of each diphthong (1), key symbols (2), and key words (3). 1 / 2 / 3 *oi,* _____ / *oi* / _____ _____, _____ / _____ / *house*

ou *kloun*	**9.** The key symbol for the vowel phoneme heard in *clown* is ______ . Rewrite *clown* to show its pronunciation. ______________
two two two no *ou* *oi*	**10.** We are recognizing _____ diphthongs. Each has _____ spellings. (How many?) (How many?) The key symbol for each diphthong is composed of _____ letters with (How many?) _____ diacritical marks. These letters will be either _____ or _____ (one, two, no) (*ou, ow*) (*oi, oy*) because they are the key symbols. We find them used in most dictionaries for pronunciation purposes.
koi *noiz* *broil* *snow* *snō* *kou*	**11.** Study the words at the right. Rewrite them using key symbols to indicate the pronunciation of all the phonemes. Underline the diphthongs. There is no diphthong in ______________ . *coy* ______________ *noise* ______________ *broil* ______________ *snow* ______________ *cow* ______________
powder, proud, *how, soil*	**12.** Underline the diphthongs in the following words. Work with care. The *ou* and *ow* often represent other phonemes. Be sure you underline only those which have the vowel phonemes found in *oil* and *house.* *powder* *proud* *course* *how* *soil* *courage* *gracious*
short	**13.** The *ous* ending, as in *gracious,* is more likely to represent the phonemes we associate with the key symbols ______________ *u* and *s* (long, short) (or the schwa and *s*) than with the diphthong *ou* and the *s.* If we do not have the word in our speaking vocabulary, however, it is difficult to determine whether the *ou* (*ow*) is a diphthong.

Review 18

1. Two of the 44 phonemes are classified as diphthongs. What are the key symbols of these two diphthongs? _____ , _____

2. The diphthongs are ____________ phonemes.
(vowel, consonant)

3. Copy the words that contain diphthongs (Write the key symbol of the diphthong following each.):

cough owl grow cow through moist oyster

4. Use key symbols to show the pronunciation of the following words; omit silent letters, underline diphthongs:

house boy ounce enjoy noise brow

(See the Answers section for the answers to Review 18.)

Vowel Digraphs

	o͞o (*food*) o͝o (*hook*)
two one	**1.** The second category of phonemes represented by two-letter vowels is that of the **vowel digraph.** A digraph is a _____-letter grapheme which represents _____ phoneme(s).
two digraph	**2.** Listen to the vowel sound as you pronounce *food* aloud. Separate the phonemes as you pronounce *food* again: *f oo d.* Say the vowel phoneme aloud. The key symbol we use to identify the vowel sound heard in *food* is o͞o. This is a _____-letter vowel grapheme representing a single phoneme. We call it a vowel ____________ .
o͞o o͞o ō ō o͞o ŭ o͞o ō ōə or ōĭ ō	**3.** Write the key symbol to indicate the pronunciation of the vowels in each of the following words. Omit silent letters. Work carefully. *school* _____ *broom* _____ *rowboat* _____ *soon* _____ *flood* _____ *through* _____ *so* _____ *poet* _____ *though* _____
no no, *flood*	**4.** Does o͞o represent the same phoneme as ō? _____ When we see *oo* in a word, can we be sure that it has the sound heard in *food?* _____ The word ____________ above contains two *os*, but has the sound of a short *u.*

Answers	Frames
no *through*	**5.** Is the sound indicated by the key symbol o͞o always spelled with two *o*s? _____ Which word in frame 3 contains /o͞o/ but is not spelled with two *o*s? ______________
ou o͞o o͞o ō o͞o o͞o o͞o o͞o *oi* ā o͞o o͞o	**6.** Examine the following words carefully. On the line following each, write the key symbol that represents its vowel-pair. *mouse* _____ *cool* _____ *kangaroo* _____ *dough* _____ *drew* _____ *due* _____ *glue* _____ *moon* _____ *coil* _____ *main* _____ *soup* _____ *cartoon* _____
yes no breve	**7.** A second digraph which cannot be represented by a single letter is found in the word *hook.* Pronounce *food,* then *hook.* Pronounce the vowel phoneme in each word. Are they spelled the same? _____ Do they sound alike? _____ Since the key symbol for the sound heard in *food* is two *o*s covered by an elongated macron (o͞o), it is logical to represent the short phoneme heard in *hook* with an elongated ______________ over the two **o** s (o͝o).
1 2 3 *oo* o͞o *food* *oo* o͝o *hook*	**8.** **A vowel digraph is a two-letter grapheme which represents one vowel phoneme.** Complete the table at the right with the most common spelling of each digraph (1), key symbol (2), and key word (3) for each digraph. 1 2 3 _____ o͞o ______________ _____ o͝o ______________
fo͝ot, go͞ose, to͝ok, lo͝ok, so͞on, po͞ol, wo͝od, to͞oth, lo͞os~~e~~	**9.** Using *food* and *hook* as key words to aid you, mark the words below to show pronunciation. *foot goose took look soon pool wood tooth loose*
digraph no *o͞o, o͝o*	**10.** When we see the vowel ______________ *oo* in a word, can we be sure of the phoneme it represents? _____ The double-*o* is most likely to represent the _____ in *food* or the _____ in *hook.* (o͞o, o͝o) (o͞o, o͝o)

Answer	Frame
goose	**11.** When you see a double-*o* in an unknown word, the only clue to pronunciation is that it most often represents the o͞o as in _____ . (*goose, book*)
	You may wish to choose other key words to help you remember the phonemes. *Hook* serves as a good key word for the phoneme we represent by o͝o if we see a resemblance between an elongated breve and a hook!
o͞o	A mental image of the flat surface of a stool may help you remember that the key symbol _____ represents the sound heard in *sto͞ol* (or a *plāte* of *fo͞od!*).
blŭd *sto͝od* *zo͞o* *flŭd* *dro͞op*	**12.** Not all *oo*'s represent the sounds heard in *food* and *hook.* Rewrite the words at the right to show the correct pronunciation of each. *blood* ___________ *stood* ___________ *zoo* ___________ *flood* ___________ *droop* ___________
phonemes consonant, vowel	**13.** The /o͞o/ and /o͝o/ represent 2 of the 44 ___________ of the American-English language. We now have identified all of the phonemes: 25 ___________ phonemes and 19 ___________ phonemes!
	However, we must study still another category of vowel combinations.

Review 19

1. What is a digraph?
2. What are the key symbols that identify each of the vowel digraphs?
3. When you see a double *o* in an unknown word, how will you know what sound it represents?
4. Using key symbols, indicate the pronunciation of each of these words: *tooth, spoon, book, loose, stood, moo, shook.*
5. Show, through the use of key symbols, how you would expect this nonsense word to be pronounced: *clood*
6. Write the symbols, consonants, and vowels to indicate the pronunciation of these words. Omit silent letters.

   boot, fudge, down, toy, shook, cocoa, night, fruit, throw, through, though, thought, quit, book, smooth, fool, breath, breathe, knight

(See the Answers section for the answers to Review 19.)

Other Vowel Pairs

grapheme phoneme /o͞o/ /o͝o/	**1.** A digraph is a ____________ composed of two letters which represent one ____________ . *oo* in *food* represents / / *oo* in *hook* represents / /
diphthongs	**2.** We have a special name for the digraphs represented by a "gliding phoneme" as found in *mouse* and *toil.* They are called _____ .
one ē ē ā ē ō ī	**3.** Now examine the following words. Each has two vowels which represent _____ phoneme(s). What phoneme does each vowel pair represent? Be sure to use the diacritical mark to identify the phoneme. _____ *rain* _____ *heat* _____ *fail* _____ *green* _____ *coat* _____ *pie*
grapheme, phoneme long	**4.** All the words in frame 3 contain a vowel digraph: Each has a two-letter ____________ which represents one ____________ ; but each of these vowel pairs represents a sound already studied: the ____________ sound we associate with a single vowel letter. None of (long, short) these pairs has a distinctive sound of its own. We will call them **vowel pairs** to distinguish them from the digraphs that represent distinctive sounds: o͞o and o͝o.
rāi̸n, three, *r, a,* *n*	**5.** We need to give further study to this large group of vowel pairs because they form one of the common patterns in the English language. First, examine the word *rain.* Underline the pair of vowels. Indicate the silent vowel by drawing a slash through it. Mark the long vowel. *Rain* has _____ phonemes represented by _____ , long _____ , and (how many?) _____ .

Answers	Frame	Words
tāi̸l sāy̸	**6.** Study the words at the right. Underline the pair of vowels in each word.	*tail* *say*
macron silent sēa̸t fēe̸d cōa̸t	As you say each word, place a ______________ over the first vowel. (macron, breve) Indicate that the second vowel is ______________ by drawing a slash through it.	*seat* *feed* *coat*
long silent	**7. A syllable must have only one vowel phoneme.** Many syllables (and one-syllable words) have two vowel letters. Note the words at the right. In these cases, the first vowel represents its ______________ sound and the second vowel is ______________ .	*rain* *feed* *hue* *toe*
two long silent	**8.** We can make a generalization about the vowel pairs in the words you have studied. When _____ vowels appear together in a syllable (or one-syllable word), the first usually represents its ______________ sound and the second is ______________ .	
bēa̸ch, plāy̸, māi̸l, ēa̸ch	**9.** Mark each vowel in these words to show the pronunciation. *beach play mail each*	
CVVC *i e* *o e* *o a* *e e*	**10.** Study the words at the right. The first two follow the pattern CVCe, the last two follow the pattern _____ . Place the vowel that represents the long sound in the first column following the word and the silent letter in the second.	*pine* _____ _____ *rose* _____ _____ *boat* _____ _____ *jeep* _____ _____
long **silent**	**11.** If the vowel pairs were as regular as those represented by the VCe ending pattern, we could form a generalization to include both types: **When there are two vowel letters in a word or syllable, the first usually represents its ______________ sound and the second is ______________ .**	

Answers	Frame	
diphthong	**12.** The generalization does not apply to *boil* because *oi* is a ______________ . It has a distinctive sound of its own.	
digraph *brŏŏk*	**13.** The generalization does not apply to *brook* because *oo* is a ______________ with a distinctive sound. Use the diacritical mark to show pronunciation. ______________	
sounded	**14.** If the only exceptions to the "first-vowel-long" generalization were the diphthongs and the double-*o* digraphs, we might consider them "phonemes represented by single letters" because in each case only one of the letters is ______________ . (silent, sounded)	
no *pail* *toe* *snow*	**15.** Study the words at the right. Can we depend upon the "first-vowel-long" generalization for all but vowel diphthongs and double-*o* digraphs? _____ Underline the words that follow the generalization: **When two vowels appear together in a word or syllable, the first usually represents the long sound and the second is silent.**	*pail* *said* *auto* *toe* *piece* *snow* *few*
silent long i̸ē i̸ē i̸ē e̸ā	**16.** Place diacritical marks on the vowel pairs in the words at the right. In this set, the first vowel is ______________ and the second represents the ______________ sound.	*field* *believe* *niece* *great*
ai, oa, ee, ea, ay	**17.** Although it is true that more words fall under the "first-vowel-long" generalization than any other, there are many exceptions. It can only be used as a clue to the possible pronunciation of a word. However, there are some pairs which follow the generalization more consistently than others. Those which are most consistent appear in these words: *rain, boat, keep, each, play.* The pairs that follow the generalization a greater percentage of the time are _____ , _____ , _____ , _____ , _____ .	

sĕd	**18.** However, even these are not without exception. One of the most common sets (*ai*) appears in *said.* Rewrite *said* using needed diacritical marks to show its pronunciation. *said* ______________

19. Indicate the pronunciation of all the vowels and consonants by using the key symbols. A part of a dictionary key is given below to provide a bit of assistance.

Answers				
nābər, bâr	*neighbor*	______________	*bear*	______________
ôt, brĕd	*ought*	______________	*bread*	______________
sô, pēs	*saw*	______________	*peace*	______________
grōn, grōō	*grown*	______________	*grew*	______________
lăf, oul	*laugh*	______________	*owl*	______________
fŏŏt, fēl	*foot*	______________	*feel*	______________

Dictionary Key

â	***care***	**ä**	***father***	**ô**	***ball, order***	**û**	***fur***
		ōō	***food***	**ŏŏ**	***hook***		

thrōō *t̸hō* *bou* *rŭf* *kôf*	no	**20.** Examine the spelling of the words at the right. They look as though they should rhyme. Do they? _____ To show the inconsistencies in our language, indicate the pronunciation of all the graphemes in these words.	*through*______________ *though*______________ *bough*______________ *rough*______________ *cough*______________

no

21. The words below seem to consist of rhyming couplets. Say the words in set 1 aloud; in set 2; set 3. Do they rhyme?______________ Indicate the pronunciation of all the graphemes in these words. Work set by set.

Answers			1		2		3	
brāk	*mōld*	*shōō*	*break*	______________	*mould*	______________	*shoe*	______________
frēk	*kŏŏd*	*tō*	*freak*	______________	*could*	______________	*toe*	______________

BOX 3.7

Diphthongs, Vowel Digraphs, and Other Vowel Pairs Study Guide

Vowel Diphthongs

Diphthong	Key Symbol	Key Word
oi, oy	*oi*	*oil*
ou, ow	*ou*	*house*

A diphthong is a single vowel phoneme, represented by two letters, resembling a glide from one sound to another. Examples of vowel diphthongs include *coin, boy, mouse,* and *how.*

Vowel Digraphs

Vowel Digraph	Key Symbol	Key Word
oo	*o͞o*	*food*
oo	*o͝o*	*hook*

A vowel digraph is a two-letter grapheme which represents one vowel phoneme. The key symbol o͞o represents the sound heard in *food* and *school,* while the key symbol o͝o represents the sound heard in *hook* and *book.*

Other Vowel Pairs

Vowel Pair	Key Symbol	Key Word
ai (rain)	*ā*	*apron*
ay (play)	*ā*	*apron*
ea (each)	*ē*	*eraser*
ee (keep)	*ē*	*eraser*
oa (boat)	*ō*	*overalls*

When two vowels appear together in a word or syllable, the first usually represents the long (glided) sound and the second is silent. Some vowel pairs follow the generalization more consistently than others. Pairs which are the most consistent appear in the words *rain, play, boat, each, keep,* and *pie.*

Answers	Frames
no	**22.** Do these sets consist of rhyming words? __________ Show their pronunciation.
	1 / 2 / 3
kou *kōm* *pād*	*cow* __________ *comb* __________ *paid* __________
lō *to͞om* *sĕd*	*low* __________ *tomb* __________ *said* __________
bŏm	*bomb* __________
though *freak, mould, toe* *low, paid*	**23.** List the words in the last three frames (20–22) that follow the "first-vowel-long" generalization.
diphthong digraph dictionary hearing	**24.** We have been working with words you know to help you to get a background. But in your reading, if you come across an unknown word with a two-vowel combination, you might first check for *ou, oi, oo,* etc., to see if it might be a __________ or a double-*o* __________ . Next, try the "first-vowel-long" generalization, since it is the most common. If that doesn't give you a clue, use your reference book, the __________ . For phonics to be of help, the word must be in your __________ vocabulary. (writing, hearing)

Review 20

1. There are many vowel pairs which follow a pattern: a d__________ has a gliding sound as _____ (key symbol) in *oil* and _____ in __________ ; a d__________ in which the _____ represents the vowel sound in *food,* and _____ in __________ .
2. Then there are pairs which do not have distinguishing key symbols because they represent single vowels which already have key symbols. For example: *boat, lean, chain.* These words contain vowel pairs which often follow the generalization:
3. The vowels may be separated as in the pattern CVCe. What is the generalization?

4. A syllable may have more than one vowel ______________ , but only one vowel ______________ .

(See the Answers section for the answers to Review 20.)

Recap II

Answers	Frames
phonemes digraphs phonemes	**1.** We have been studying 44 ______________ (sound units) of the American-English language. The consonants fell into two groups: the 18 represented by single letters and the 7 ______________ . The 19 vowel ______________ also fall into groups, 15 represented by single vowel letters and 4 by two-letter combinations.
short long	**2.** We put our greatest emphasis on the five ______________ sounds (as in *hop*), and the five ______________ sounds (as in *hope*). (As you work through these frames, complete the outline at the right. Write the diacritical marks for the short vowels in I.A., and the diacritical marks for the long vowels in I.B.)
ə unaccented schwa	**3.** We use a nonletter symbol (______) to designate the soft sound heard in the ______________ syllable of many two- or three-syllable words. We call it the ______________ . (Fill in C.1.)
r *câre, ärm, ôt,* *hûrt*	**4.** There are four other single-letter phonemes which are often controlled by the letter following them, generally *l, w,* or _____ . These phonemes represent a large variety of graphemes (e.g., *â* may represent *ai, a, ei, e, ea, ay*) in various words. Mark the four key symbols in this sentence: *Take care of your arm, you ought not hurt it.* (C.2, 3, 4, 5.)
diphthongs *oi ou* *house*	**5.** We also studied four vowel phonemes represented by two vowel letters. Two of these are gliding sounds called ______________ . They are represented by _______ in *oil* and _____ in ______________ . (Part II A.)

Vowel phonemes represented by

- I. Single letter symbols
  - A. Short
    1. ă
    2.
    3.
    4.
    5.
  - B. Long
    1.
    2. ē
    3.
    4.
    5.
  - C. Other
    1.
    2. â
    3.
    4.
    5.
- II. Double letter symbols
  - A. Diphthongs
    1.
    2.
  - B. Digraphs
    1.
    2.

digraphs o͞o, o͝o	**6.** The other two-letter combinations with distinctive sounds needed to complete the 19 vowel phonemes are called ______________ . They are found in _____ as in *food* and _____ as in *hook.* You have now completed the outline of the key symbols that represent the vowel phonemes. Turn to page 153 to correct. Use the outline, right-hand side, beginning with No. 26. You have mastered all the phonemes!
symbols ōa̸, ēe̸, ēa̸, āi̸ ō, ē, ē, ā long, silent	**7.** There are other vowel pairs which do not have distinguishing key ______________ because they represent single vowels with their own phonemes. For example: *coat, fleet, dean, main.* What vowel phoneme is represented in each of these? _____ , _____ , _____ , _____ . Mark the vowels in each word. In general, the first vowel represents its ______________ sound and the second of the pair is ______________ .
ō, ŏ ə, ô, û y, ĭ silent *a, e, e* listening	**8.** Vowel letters are not very reliable. **a.** A letter may represent more than one phoneme: For example, an *o* may represent _____ as in *hope,* _____ as in *hop,* _____ as in *mammoth,* _____ as in *ought,* _____ as in *worm.* **b.** A phoneme may be represented by more than one vowel letter: The *ĭ* may be represented by _____ in *myth,* _____ in *fin,* _____. **c.** A letter may represent no phoneme, it may be _____ as the _____ in *roam,* the _____ in *race,* the _____ in *doe.* Although vowels are not very reliable, the use of certain generalizations will help us to identify words already in our ______________ vocabulary. (reading, writing, listening) (Of course, there are exceptions to the generalizations, too!)

long, silent	**9.** Some of these generalizations have been referred to above, others follow. When a one-syllable word or accented syllable contains two vowels, one of which is the final *e,* the first vowel usually represents its ____________ sound and the final *e* is ____________ (the VCe pattern).
phoneme *echo, say, though, into* consonant *open, thought, rate, once* hearing the final phoneme	**10.** An open syllable ends with a vowel ____________ (the CV pattern). (phoneme, letter) Underline the words that end with an open syllable: *echo, open, say, though, thought, rate, into, once.* A closed syllable ends with a ____________ phoneme (the VC pattern). Which of the words above have closed syllables? Whether a syllable is open or closed depends upon ________________________ . (hearing the final phoneme, seeing the final letter)
long *he, why* CV	**11.** A single vowel in an open accented syllable often represents its ____________ sound. Which words follow this generalization? *he, why, pen, road, do* The vowel-consonant pattern is ____________ .
short *pin, sent, cat* VC	**12.** A single vowel in a closed accented syllable usually represents its ____________ sound. Which words follow this generalization? *pin, sent, cat, hope, thought* The vowel-consonant pattern is ____________ .
never (at least in English words) yes	**13.** Is *y* a vowel or a consonant? The vowel *y* ____________ (always, never, you can't tell) comes at the beginning of a word. Is the above true of a vowel *w?* _____
phoneme, vowel	**14.** Although a syllable may have more than one letter, it has only one vowel ____________ . The ____________ has the most influence on the syllable. (vowel, consonant)

accented ə (*schwa*)	**15.** Vowels behave differently in accented and unaccented syllables. The vowel is most clearly heard in the ____________ syllable. The vowel in most unaccented syllables represents the _____ or the ĭ.
mē lēpe̸, phā tŏg, *rĕl nō, phō, ŏt,* *drāi̸f, skōōs*	**16.** The generalizations we have studied in connection with these vowel phonemes should aid in the pronunciation of words we do not recognize. The words below are nonsense words. Take a chance that the vowel phonemes follow the rules even in unaccented syllables or have their most common sound. Mark every vowel in these "words" to show pronunciation: *me lepe* *pha tog* *rel no* *pho* *ot* *draif* *skoos*

Part IV

A Review of the Phonemes

phonemes (or sounds)	**1.** Our written language is not based on pictorial representations of objects or ideas. It is a phonetic language in that there is a relationship between the letters of the alphabet and the ____________ of the spoken language.
consonants	**2.** In fact, many of the ____________ are fairly reliable as to sound. (consonants, vowels)
phonemes letters	**3.** However, there are so many inconsistencies in the sound-letter relationship that the English language is not an easy one to learn to read. If it were a consistent, strictly phonetic language, then (1) there would be one and only one letter to represent each of the ____________ of the spoken language; (2) there would be one and only one phoneme represented by each of the ____________ of the alphabet.

26 phonemes phonemes *sh* silent	**4.** The truth of the matter is: (1) **A letter may represent more than one sound.** For example, each vowel represents several sounds. Our alphabet has _____ letters (and some of them are useless) to represent the 44 ______________ . (2) **The same sound may be represented by more than one letter.** The 44 ______________ are represented by 251 different graphemes. For example, we spell the first consonant phoneme we hear in *chute* (key symbol: _____) in 14 different ways! (3) **A letter may represent no sound.** Almost any letter may, at some time or another, be ______________ .
spoken	**5.** We have identified the 44 phonemes that, for all practical purposes in the teaching of reading, make up the sounds of our ____________ (spoken, written) language.
symbol *j*	**6.** We have designated a key symbol for each of these phonemes to serve as our pronunciation guide. These key pronunciation symbols, then, provide us with a one-to-one correspondence between sound and ______________ . For example, we use the _____ to symbolize the sound heard in *jam,* even though it may be represented by *g* as in *gentle, d* as in *graduate,* or *dg* as in *judgment.*
key symbols	**7.** Let us review, through the following outline, the 44 phonemes we have identified and the ______________ ______________ we have designated for each. Study and make responses as indicated. When choices appear in parentheses, underline the correct answer. For example, there are 44 (phonemes, graphemes).

Review Outline

	I. CONSONANT PHONEMES	Key Symbol
	A. Represented by a single consonant letter	
boat	*b* as in (*boat, comb*). (Select the word in which *b* represents the sound we associate with its key symbol.)	1. *b*
k	(*c* represents either the _____ (*come*) or the	
s	_____ (*city*). It has no phoneme of its own, therefore no key symbol.)	
dog	*d* as in (*dog, jumped*).	2. *d*
	f as in *fish.* (This phoneme is sometimes spelled	3. *f*
gh, ph	_____ as in *enough,* or _____ as in *graph.*)	
hard	*g* as in *goat.* (This is called the [soft, hard] sound. It is the sound usually heard when followed by the vowels	4. *g*
a, o, u	_____, _____, and _____ and when followed by any other consonant or appearing at the end of the word.)	
hat	*h* as in (*ghost, hat, honor*).	5. *h*
	j as in *jeep.* (This phoneme is often represented by a	6. *j*
e, i, y	*g* followed by the vowels _____, _____, or _____.)	
	k as in *kite.* (This phoneme is often represented by a *c*	7. *k*
a, o, u	followed by the vowels _____, _____, or _____. It is	
q	also represented by a _____ as in *queen.*)	
lion	*l* as in (*lion, calm*).	8. *l*
reliable	*m* as in *moon* is a very (reliable, unreliable) letter.	9. *m*
nut	*n* as in (*condemn, nut*).	10. *n*

		Key Symbol
pig	*p* as in (*graph, pig*).	11. *p*
k	(*q* has no key symbol. The dictionary always uses a _____ to indicate its pronunciation.)	
reliable	*r* as in *ring. R* is very (reliable, unreliable).	12. *r*
sun	*s* as in (*his, sure, sun*). (Select the word in which the *s* represents its key symbol phoneme.)	13. *s*
table	*t* as in (*table, than*).	14. *t*
w	(*u* sometimes serves as the consonant _____ . This is generally true when it follows *q*.)	
van	*v* as in (*van, off*).	15. *v*
wagon	*w* as in (*two, why, wagon, who*).	16. *w*
ks	(*x* has no phoneme of its own. It has the sound represented by the *gz*, the _____ , or the *z*.)	
yo-yo	*y* as in (*yo-yo, day*).	17. *y*
zipper	*z* as in (*zipper, quartz*).	18. *z*
	B. Represented by consonant digraphs	
chair (The other two have symbols *k* and *sh*.)	*ch* as in (*chair, choir, machine*).	19. *ch*
f	(*gh* has no phoneme of its own. It often represents the key symbol _____ as in *enough*.)	
king	*ng* as in (*congest, king*).	20. *ng*
f	(*ph* has no phoneme of its own. The key symbol _____ commonly represents the sound, as in *phone*.)	
shoe	*sh* as in (*shoe, division*).	21. *sh*
thumb	*th* as in (*thumb, Thomas*).	22. *th*

		Key Symbol
that	*th* as in (*think, that*).	23. *t̸h*
whale	*wh* as in (*who, whale*).	24. *wh*
treasure (*Edge* has the *j* key symbol.)	*zh* as in (*treasure, edge*).	25. *zh*
	II. VOWEL PHONEMES	
	A. Represented by single vowel letters	
	1. Short sounds	
apple	*a* as in (*date, apple, all*).	26. *ă*
elephant	*e* as in (*beat, pine, elephant*).	27. *ĕ*
igloo	*i* as in (*igloo, pine, rind*).	28. *ĭ*
ox	*o* as in (*orb, ox*).	29. *ŏ*
umbrella	*u* as in (*umbrella, full*).	30. *ŭ*
	(*y*, as a vowel, has no distinctive sound of its own.	
short i	It can have the key symbol of the _____ _____ as in *hymn*.)	
	2. Long sounds	
apron	*a* as in (*apron, cat*).	31. *ā*
eraser	*e* as in (*fed, eraser*).	32. *ē*
ice	*i* as in (*ill, ice*).	33. *ī*
overalls	*o* as in (*overalls, not*).	34. *ō*
unicorn	*u* as in (*unicorn, us*).	35. *ū*
	(*y* has no vowel phoneme of its own. Its key symbol	
ī, ĭ	can be the _____ as in *my*, the _____ as in *myth*,	
ē	and the _____ as in *happy*.)	

		Key Symbol
a, e, i o, u	**3. Other single vowel sounds** ə represents the soft, unaccented sound of the vowel _____ in *comma,* _____ in *chicken,* _____ in *family,* _____ in *button,* _____ in *circus.*	36. ə
care, chair, there	â as in *care, chair, there* . . . All of these and those following are examples; underline the parts that represent the sounds.	37. â
father, hearth, sergeant	ä as in *father, hearth, sergeant* . . .	38. ä
order, tall, fault	ô as in *order, tall, fault* . . .	39. ô
hurt, term, courage	û as in *hurt, term, courage* . . .	40. û
oy ow	**B. Represented by vowel combinations** **1. Diphthongs** *oi* as in *oil.* This phoneme is also represented by the letters _____ . *ou* as in *house.* This phoneme is often represented by the vowels _____ .	41. *oi* 42. *ou*
food *hook*	**2. Vowel digraphs** o͞o as in (*food, flood*). o͝o as in (*food, flood, hook*).	43. o͞o 44. o͝o
	3. Other vowel pairs The key symbols for other vowel pairs—*ai, oa,* and so forth—have already been given.	
44	**4.** Take another look at the key symbol column on these last pages. We have accounted for the _____ phonemes with which we are concerned in teaching reading! They may be represented by other spellings—but these are the basic sounds of the American-English language. Now review the headings of the outline just given.	

Part V

Syllabication and Accent

pronunciation	1. **The syllable is the unit of pronunciation.** It is convenient to use one-syllable words to illustrate the vowel and consonant phonemes because a one-syllable word is, in itself, one unit of ____________ .
syllable	2. The generalizations that apply to a one-syllable word may apply to each syllable of a two-or-more syllable word and generally apply to the accented ____________ of a word.
syllable	3. **There is one vowel phoneme in each unit of pronunciation,** that is, in each ____________ .
vowel two	4. Each syllable contains only one ____________ phoneme. If you hear two vowel phonemes, you may be sure the word has ________ syllables.

---

phoneme

pine ī

boy oi

right ī

pause ô

(If you missed *pause* ô, reread the frame.)

5. Each syllable may have more than one vowel letter but only one vowel _____________ .

The word *cause* (kôz) has one vowel phoneme: ô. Underline the vowel letters in the words at the right. Write the key symbol that represents the vowel phoneme in the space following each word; mark it to show pronunciation.

pine _____

boy _____

right _____

pause _____

---

syllables

1	ĕ	
1	ŭ	(*jŭmpt*)
2	ă	ĭ (or ə)
2	ā	ĭ
1	ou	

6. How many units of pronunciation (or _____________) are there in each of these words? What is the vowel phoneme in each syllable? Mark the vowel(s), in the space at the right, to show pronunciation.

	No. of Syllables	*Vowel Phoneme(s)*
red	_____	_____________
jumped	_____	_____________
candid	_____	_____________
raining	_____	_____________
house	_____	_____________

---

syllable

7. **One syllable in a two-or-more syllable word receives more emphasis or greater stress than the other syllables.**

We indicate this accented _____________ by placing an accent mark (′) at the end of the accented syllable.

---

accent (or stress)

8. **In multisyllabic words, more than one syllable may be stressed.**

There will be one primary _____________ (shown by ′) and one or more secondary accents. The secondary accent is shown by ′.

---

vowel

9. We have already noted that accent, or stress point, affects

_____________ sounds.
(vowel, consonant)

accented	**10. The vowel phoneme is the most prominent part of the syllable. Vowels behave differently in accented and unaccented syllables.** The vowel is most clearly heard in the ______ syllable.
schwa	**11.** Many syllables, when pronounced carefully in isolation, appear to follow the generalizations we have noted. In normal speech, however, we have a tendency to give most vowels in the unaccented syllables the soft, short, indistinct ______ sound.
ŏ ə	**12.** We can clearly see this behavior of vowels in accented and unaccented syllables in words that are spelled alike but accented differently. Read these sentences: *Your conduct is exemplary. (k ___ n′dukt)* *I will conduct you through the factory. (k ___ n dukt′)* Show the pronunciation of the vowel in each of the first syllables above.
kŏn′ *kən* *kəm* *kŏm′*	**13.** Write the first syllable of each of the underlined words to show its pronunciation. If the first syllable is the stressed syllable, include the accent mark. *I signed the contract.* ______ *"Can't" is a contraction.* ______ *The work is complete.* ______ *You are competent!* ______
phoneme letter	**14.** Each syllable has only one vowel ______ (phoneme, letter). It may have more than one vowel ______ (phoneme, letter).
yes yes yes *oi,* diphthong	**15.** Is *boy* a one-syllable word? ______ Does it have more than one vowel letter? ______ Does it have one vowel phoneme? ______ What key symbol represents this phoneme? ___ This vowel phoneme is called a ______ .

accent	**16.** To decode a word not known at sight, we need to have some idea of where to place the accent. There are some clues to where the ____________ may be found in unknown words.

Clues to Placement of Accent

accent	**1.** Obviously, it is necessary to have some understanding of where to expect to find the accented syllable. **First, we consider one-syllable words to have a primary ____________ .**	
yes (They are one-syllable words; therefore, they are the accented syllable.)	**2.** The vowel phoneme in the accented syllable tends to follow the generalizations we have studied concerning its sound. Would you expect the words at the right to conform to these generalizations? ____________	*met* *rain* *rate* *cat* *hope* *boy*
accented	**3.** Dictionaries, in showing pronunciation, do not place accent marks on one-syllable words. It is taken for granted that they are ____________ .	
ex chang′ ing *play′ ful* *slow′ ly* *cold′ est*	**4.** **In general, prefixes and suffixes (affixes) form separate syllables. The accent usually falls on or within the root word.** Place the accents in these words.	*ex chang ing* *play ful* *slow ly* *cold est*
suffix	**5.** The root word is more likely to be accented than the prefix or ____________ .	

Answers	Frames
accent snow′ man some′ thing cow′ boy	**6.** **In compound words, the primary ____________ usually falls on or within the first "word."** Rewrite these compound words to show the syllables; place the accents. *snowman* ____________ *something* ____________ *cowboy* ____________
black bird′ *black′bird*	**7.** Accent within sentences will not be considered here. However, note that a change in accent in the following sentences changes the meaning. Place the accent on *black* or *bird* in each sentence: *I see a black bird; I think it is a crow.* *The blackbird built its nest in the marsh.*
root first	**8.** We have noted that (1) one-syllable words are accented; (2) accents usually fall on or within the ____________ word rather than on an affix; (3) the ____________ "word" in a compound word is usually the accented one.
first second first second	**9.** **The place of the accent may differentiate between a noun and a verb in words that are spelled alike:** *What is this object?* ____________ *Do you object?* ____________ *This is a present for you.* ____________ *Please present this to your friend.* ____________ **The accents usually fall on the first syllables of nouns.** Study the above sentences. Write first or second to show the syllable on which the accent falls in each of the underlined words.
be gin′ ning *mil′ lion* *din′ ner*	**10.** **When there is a double consonant within a word, the accent usually falls on the syllable that closes with the first letter of the double consonant:** *lat′ter.* *be gin ning* *mil lion* *din ner* Place the accents in these words.

Answers	Frame	Words
con di′ tion *car na′ tion* *ex ag ger a′ tion* *di rec′ tion*	11. **In most multisyllabic words ending in *tion,* the primary accent falls on the syllable preceding the *tion* ending.** Example: *del e ga′ tion.* Place the primary accents in these words.	*con di tion* *car na tion* *ex ag ger a tion* *di rec tion*
main tain′ *be neath′* *ex plain′*	12. **When the vowel phoneme in the last syllable of a word is composed of two vowel letters, that syllable is most often accented.** Mark the accents in these words.	*main tain* *be neath* *ex plain*
first consonant vowel *tion*	13. We have noted that (1) when a word is used as different parts of speech, the accent is usually on the ____________ syllable of the noun; (2) the accent usually falls on the syllable that closes with the first letter of a double ____________ ; (3) when the last (and closed) syllable of a word has two ____________ letters, that syllable is accented; and (4) the accent falls on the syllable preceding the ____________ ending.	
fin′ ish *prac′ tice* *scoun′ drel* *cen′ ter* *mon′ key* *lis′ ten*	14. **When there is no other clue, note that the accent most often falls on the first syllable of a two-syllable word.** Study these words to see if they follow this generalization. Place the accents.	*fin ish* *prac tice* *scoun drel* *cen ter* *mon key* *lis ten*
accented	15. Let us review all the generalizations concerning the placement of the accent. Consider the word *day.* A one-syllable word is considered to be ____________ . (accented, unaccented)	
sun′ set compound first	16. Rewrite the word *sunset* and place the accent: ____________ . In ____________ words, the accent usually falls on the ____________ "word."	

catch' ing root prefix	**17.** Rewrite the word *catching* and place the accent: ____________ . The accent usually falls on the ____________ word rather than on the suffix or ____________ .
un faith' ful root	**18.** Consider this word: *unfaithful.* Place the accent. Sometimes a root word has more than one affix, or the word has so many syllables that two or more syllables are stressed. The primary accent, then, usually falls on or within the ____________ word.
reb' el noun	**19.** Consider the word *rebel* in the sentence: *He is a rebel.* Place the accent: ____________ . Certain words which are spelled the same sometimes function as different parts of speech. The accent on the first syllable generally indicates that it is a ____________ .
re gret' ta ble consonant closes consonant	**20.** Consider this word: *re gret ta ble.* Place the accent. When there is a double ____________ within a word, the accent usually falls on the syllable that ____________ (closes, opens) with the first letter of the double ____________ .
con tain' last	**21.** Consider this word: *con tain.* Place the accent. When two vowel letters appear within the last syllable of a two-syllable word, the ____________ (first, last) syllable is most often accented.

BOX 5.1

Syllable Accent Study Guide

Syllable Defined

The syllable is the unit of pronunciation. There is one vowel phoneme in each syllable (unit of pronunciation). Each syllable may have more than one vowel letter but only one vowel phoneme (*boy, pause*).

Accent or Stress

One syllable in a two-or-more syllable word receives more emphasis or greater stress than the other syllables. Accent, or stress point, affects the vowel sound.

Accent Marks

An accent mark indicates the primary stress (*ti′ ger*). In multisyllabic words, more than one syllable may be stressed. The secondary accent is shown by (′) (*cent′ ti pede′*).

Vowels in Accented Syllables

Vowels behave differently in accented and unaccented syllables. The vowel is most clearly heard in the accented syllable (*pa′ per, plan′ et*).

Vowels in Unaccented Syllables

We have a tendency to give most vowels in the unaccented syllables the soft, short, indistinct *schwa* sound (*pen′ cil, pĕn′ səl*), or the short i (*bracelet, brās′ lĭt*).

Clues to Placement of Accent

One-syllable Words We consider one-syllable words to have a primary accent (*bed′, boy′*).

Prefixes and Suffixes In general, prefixes and suffixes (affixes) form separate syllables. The accent usually falls on or within the root word (*play′ ful, slow′ ly*).

Compound Words In compound words, the primary accent usually falls on or within the first "word" (*cup′ cake, snow′ man*).

Nouns and Verbs The place of the accent may differentiate between a noun and a verb in words that are spelled alike. The accent usually falls on the first syllable of nouns (*ob′ ject*) and the second syllable of verbs (*ob ject′*). (*His con′ duct was excellent. He will con duct′ the tour.*)

Double Consonants When there is a double consonant within a word, the accent usually falls on the syllable that closes the first letter of the double consonant (*let′ ter, yel′ low*).

Words Ending with tion In most polysyllabic words ending in *tion,* the primary accent falls on the syllable preceding the *tion* spelling (*na′ tion, di rec′ tion*).

Two Vowels in the Final Syllable When the vowel phoneme in the last syllable of a word is composed of two vowel letters, that syllable is most often accented (*ex plain′, be neath′*).

When There Is No Clue to Accent When there is no other clue, the accent most often falls on the first syllable of a two-syllable word (*fin′ ish, prac′ tice*).

for get′ ting *con′ tract* *de mand′ ed* *ap pear′ ance* *o′ pen ing* *can teen′* *show′ boat*	**22.** Using what information you have and remembering that it is not customary to place accent marks on one-syllable words, place accent marks in all the appropriate places in the following: *I was for get ting my con tract which de mand ed my ap pear ance at the o pen ing of the can teen on the show boat.*

Review 21

1. The unit of pronunciation is the ____________ .
2. The basic speech sound, or the smallest sound-bearing unit, is the ____________ .
3. Can there be more than one vowel letter in a syllable?
4. Can there be more than one vowel sound in a syllable?
5. The vowel phoneme is most clearly heard in the ____________ syllable.
6. We studied several generalizations concerning the placement of accent marks. State the generalization that applies to each of these words. Place the primary accent in each word.

a. *in ter change a ble*	**e.** *na tion*
b. *cow boy*	**f.** *dol lar*
c. *fast*	**g.** *con ceal*
d. *ex′ port; ex port′*	**h.** *pa per*

(See the Answers section for the answers to Review 21.)

Clues to Syllable Division

A single vowel in a closed syllable generally represents its short sound.	**1.** We have established some guidelines to help us decide upon which syllable an accent might fall. We still have this problem: Where do the syllabic divisions occur? There are generalizations to help but with many exceptions. First, we need to review two generalizations concerning vowel phonemes. State the generalization that applies to the vowel sound of *met.*
A single vowel in an open syllable generally represents its long sound.	**2.** State the generalization that applies to the vowel sound of *me* and *so.*
short (unglided)	**3.** Let us attempt to syllabicate the word *pupil.* If you divided it *pup il,* the first vowel would be expected to have its ____________ sound.
long (glided), open	**4.** If you divided it *pu pil,* the first vowel would be expected to have its ____________ sound: It is in a(n) ____________ syllable. (open, closed)
last (unaccented) *pū′pəl*	**5.** Write the correct pronunciation of *pupil,* placing the accent and using the *schwa* in the ____________ syllable. ____________
When there is no other clue in a two-syllable word, the accent most often falls on the first syllable.	**6.** Which generalization concerning placement of accent would seem to apply?

pu pil (pū′pəl)	**7.** Now write *pupil* as it would appear in the dictionary. The entry word should show syllabication only. Follow this by rewriting the word to show pronunciation, using the key symbols and omitting silent letters (if any). ____________ ____________
vowel	**8.** Let us make a generalization: **If the first vowel in a two-syllable word is followed by a single consonant, that consonant often begins the second syllable.** In other words, the syllable division is between the single ____________ and the single consonant.
si lent (sī′ lənt) *ti ger (tī′ gər)* *lo cal (lō′ kəl)*	**9.** Follow the above generalization and write these words as they would appear in the dictionary entry word followed by pronunciation. *silent* ____________ ____________ *tiger* ____________ ____________ *local* ____________ ____________
silent	**10.** Let us review another generalization: When two like consonants appear together, the second is generally ____________ .
short (unglided) long (glided) short (unglided)	**11.** Examine the word *puppet.* If we divide it *pup pet,* we would expect the first vowel to have its ____________ sound. If we divide it *pu ppet,* we would expect the *u* to be ____________ . The *u* in the word *puppet* should be ____________ .
closed *pŭp pet*	**12.** For the *u* to have the correct sound in the word *puppet,* it should appear in a(n) ____________ syllable. Write the word *puppet* (closed, open) dividing it correctly. Mark the *u.* ____________

pup pet (pŭp′ ət or pŭp′ ĭt) *p* short	**13.** Now write *puppet* as it would appear in the dictionary—first the entry word, using syllabication but the correct spelling. ________ ________ (________ ________) Follow this with the correct pronunciation. Omit the second _____ . Sometimes in an unaccented syllable the vowel is not a *schwa* but rather a related sound, the soft ____________ *i.* (short, long)
 consonants **consonants**	**14.** We can make a generalization: **When two vowel letters are separated by two ____________ ,** **the syllable division is generally between the ____________ .**
 open long (glided) first	**15.** Note the relationship between the sounds of the vowels, the syllabication, and the accent. We divided the word *pupil;* the first syllable is a(n) ____________ (open, closed) syllable with the division between the vowel and the consonant. The vowel has its ____________ sound, and the accent is on the ____________ syllable.
closed short first	**16.** Then we divided *puppet.* The first letters are the same, but the pronunciation is different: The first syllable is ____________ , the sound represented by the first vowel is ____________ , and the accent is on the ____________ syllable.
 closed short	**17.** The syllabic division between consonants is more dependable than the division between the single vowel and single consonant. There are many words in which the first single consonant ends the first syllable: *ex it, nov ice, hon or, fac et.* In these words, the first syllable is ____________ and the vowel has (open, closed) its ____________ sound.

second	**18.** When in doubt, however, try the generalization first: **If the first vowel in a two-syllable word is followed by a single consonant, that consonant often begins** **the ____________ syllable,** as in *pu pil.*
tī ger yes	**19.** Divide *tiger* into syllables: _____ _____ . Mark the vowel in the first syllable to show pronunciation. If *tiger* were spelled with two *g*'s, would it be expected to rhyme with *bigger?* ____________
lĕt′ ter yes *nŭm′ ber* *ĕf′ fort* yes *shăl′ low* yes	**20.** Study the words at the right. Is each a two-or-more syllable word? _____ Is there a single vowel in the first syllable? _____ Is the single vowel followed by two consonants? _____ *letter* _____ _____ *number* _____ _____ *effort* _____ _____ *shallow* _____ _____ If so, divide the words between the consonants. Mark the first vowel in each to show its pronunciation. Mark the accent.
If the first vowel in a two-syllable word is followed by a single consonant, that consonant often begins the second syllable.	**21.** State the generalization for the syllabication of *meter.*
When two vowel letters are separated by two consonants, generally the word is divided between the consonants.	**22.** State the generalization for the syllabication of *member.*

Answers	Frames
hōpe̸ *hŏp* *hŏp′ p̸ĭng* long	**23.** Show the pronunciation of these words by dividing them into syllables, marking the vowels, placing the accents, and drawing a slash through silent letters. *hope* __________ *hop* __________ *hopping* __________ If we did not double the *p* to form *hopping,* we might expect the last letter of the first syllable to represent a __________ (long, short) *o.* This would not be our intention.
th	**24.** Remember that a two-letter grapheme, a digraph, acts as a single letter. **Do not syllabicate between letters of a digraph.** The word *together* is not *to get her* because the digraph ______ is not to be divided.
slŭg′ gish, rĕs′ pite *mē′ ter, lā′ ter* *mō′ tive, lăt′ ter* *yes*	**25.** We are studying generalizations which pertain to syllabication. In this study we are using words we already know. Now pretend you do not know the words below. Divide them into syllables following the "open-syllable, long" and "closed-syllable, short" generalizations. Mark the vowel in the first syllable to show pronunciation. Place the accent. *sluggish* __________ *respite* __________ *meter* __________ *later* __________ *motive* __________ *latter* __________ Are all of these words marked the way they really are pronounced? __________
pī′ rate, rī′ gid *drā′ gon, tĕm′ per a ture′*	**26.** Pretend you do not know the words below. Syllabicate them according to the generalizations we've been studying. Mark the first vowel. Place the accent. Follow the directions carefully. *pirate* __________ *rigid* __________ *dragon* __________ *temperature* __________

no rĭg′ id, drăg′ on	**27.** Reread the words in the previous frame. Are they all marked the way they are really pronounced? ________ . If any are not, correctly divide them into syllables and mark the vowel in the first syllable. Place the accent: ________ , ________
often	**28.** If the first vowel is followed by a single consonant, that consonant ________ begins the second syllable. (always, often) (Take time to check your results. Are you getting them all correct? Are you applying what you have learned? Do you complete a frame, writing all the answers before you move the mask down? You should be able to see the results of your study. May you have a great feeling of self-satisfaction!)
root syllables	**29.** We have observed that the accent is generally on the _____ word rather than on the prefix or suffix. It is natural, then, to expect prefixes and suffixes to form ________ separate from the root word.
de lay *re lent less* *re o pen ing*	**30.** **Prefixes and suffixes usually form separate syllables from the root word.** Divide the words at the right into syllables. *delay* ________ *relentless* ________ *reopening* ________
sī′ dər *sō′ də* *stā′ shən* *ŭn tīm′ lē* *wĭn′ dō*	**31.** Observing the generalizations, divide the words at the right into syllables and mark them to show pronunciation. Place the accents. *cider* ________ *soda* ________ *station* ________ *untimely* ________ *window* ________
ble two *cle* *ble*	**32.** Examine the words *table, circle, marble.* Each of these words has ________ syllables. Write the last syllable in each word. We can show the pronunciation of these syllables as *bəl, kəl.* *ta* _____ *cir* _____ *mar* _____

consonant	**33.** A helpful generalization is: **If the last syllable of a word ends in *le* preceded by a ____________, that consonant usually begins the last syllable.**
ga ble (gā′ bəl)	**34.** Write the complete pronunciation of *gable* as it would appear in the dictionary. _____ _____ (_____ _____)
pronunciation (*Meaning* is correct also.)	**35.** Now let us examine a word which is the same as *gable* except for an *m* which precedes the *ble*. Read this sentence: *Do not gamble with your health.* The letter *m* affects the ____________ of the word.
b *gam ble*	**36.** The last syllable in *gamble* ends with *le* preceded by the consonant _____. Show how we would divide the word. (Note that other generalizations correctly apply to these words.) *gamble* ____________
gam ble (găm′ bəl)	**37.** Now write *gamble* as it would appear in the dictionary. ____________ ____________ (____________ ____________)
long	**38.** **We have noted that the clues to the pronunciation of a given word are:** **a. the vowel phonemes** **b. the consonant phonemes** **c. the position of the vowel in the syllable** **d. the syllable accented** If the vowel is the last and only letter in the syllable, it usually has its ____________ sound.

consonants consonant root diphthong	**39.** Syllable divisions are most commonly made: a. between two ____________ (as in *ladder*) b. between a single vowel and a single ____________ (as in *paper*) c. between prefixes, suffixes, and ____________ words. They are not made between letters representing a single phoneme, that is, between the letters of a digraph or a ____________ (as *appoint*).
syllable are not	**40.** We have seen that syllables are units of pronunciation. The arrangement of vowels and consonants within the ____________ affects the pronunciation. We have noted that generalizations about syllabication are helpful but ____________ infallible. (are, are not)
ā′ bəl *change a ble* *chānj′ ə bəl*	**41.** Sounds may change with the lengthening of the word: Divide *able* into syllables. Mark it to show pronunciation. ____________ Divide *changeable* into syllables. ____________________ Rewrite it to show pronunciation. ____________________
long *schwa* unaccented	**42.** In *able* the *a* represents the ____________ sound. In *changeable* the second *a* represents the ____________ sound; it is now in the ____________ syllable. (accented, unaccented)
Cv̆C Cv̆ph vC CvC blv̄ Cv̄ Cvph Cv̄phe̸ Did you succeed?	**43.** To check our understanding, let us use symbols. Study the key below at the left. Divide the "words" in the right column into syllables, marking the vowels as they would be found most commonly and as though all syllables were accented. Key: C is consonant v is vowel (other than *e*) e̸ is silent *e* ph is digraph bl is cluster which is blended C v C C v ph v C C v C bl v C v C v ph C v ph e̸

BOX 5.2

Syllable Division Study Guide

Four Clues to Pronunciation

The four important clues to the pronunciation of a given word are (1) the vowel phonemes, (2) the consonant phonemes, (3) the position of the vowel in the syllable, and (4) the accented syllable.

First Vowel Followed by a Single Consonant

If the first vowel in a two-syllable word is followed by a single consonant, that consonant often begins the second syllable (*ti′ ger, si′ lent*).

Two Vowels Separated by Two Consonants

When two vowels are separated by two consonants, the syllable division is generally between the consonants (*pup′ pet, plan′ et*). Syllable division between consonants is more dependable than the division between the single vowel and single consonant.

Consonant Digraphs

Do not syllabicate between digraphs (*to geth′ er,* not *to get her*).

Prefixes and Suffixes

In general, prefixes and suffixes form separate syllables from the root word (*play′ ful, un smil′ ing*).

Last Syllable *le:*

If the last syllable of a word ends in *le* preceded by a consonant, that consonant usually begins the last syllable (*ta′ ble, han′ dle*).

Review 22

1. Examine the following consonant-vowel word patterns. Place a slash where the syllable division would be most likely to occur. Make sure that there is a vowel in each syllable. Give the reason you divided the word as you did. There are no digraphs in these words.
   a. CVCVCC
   b. CVCCVC
   c. CVCCV
   d. CCVCVCC
2. How would you expect the following words to be divided? Why? (Pretend that you do not know the words; then you cannot say, "I can hear the pronunciation unit.")
   a. *respectful*
   b. *capable*
   c. *father*

   (See the Answers section for the answers to Review 22.)

Part VI

Onset and Rime

	at *ight* *old* *ig*
26 44 vowels, consonants	**1.** Thus far we have been studying the _____ graphemes and _____ phonemes of the American-English language. We have learned that the arrangement of _____ and _____ within the syllable affects the pronunciation.
consonant begins	**2.** We will now turn our attention to the consonant(s) at the beginning of the syllable, and the vowel and the consonant(s) that follow it at the end of the syllable. The **onset** is the ____________ letter(s) that precedes the vowel in a syllable. The dictionary defines an onset as a beginning or commencement. Therefore, a syllable ____________ with an onset. (begins, ends)
single consonant blend digraph	**3.** The onset is the single consonant, consonant blend, or consonant digraph that begins a syllable. Study these words: *boil, street, thorn.* The onset in *boil* is a ____________ . (single consonant, consonant blend) The onset in *street* is a consonant ____________ . (blend, digraph) The onset in *thorn* is a consonant ____________ . (blend, digraph)

pig, smile, chip, wish, splash, bold, strain, pill three	**4.** Underline the onset in the one-syllable words below. Count the letters in each of the onsets you underline. *pig smile chip wish splash bold strain pill* You can see that there are from one to ____________ consonant (How many?) letters in an onset.
c, k, *cat* kn, n, *knight* bl, bl, *black* gh, g, *ghost* ph, f, *phone* wh, wh, *white* sk, sk, *skin* p, p, *pink* consonant	**5.** Complete the table by filling in the onset (1) and key symbol (2) for each one-syllable word (3). 1 2 3 ____ ____ *cat* ____ ____ *knight* ____ ____ *black* ____ ____ *ghost* ____ ____ *phone* ____ ____ *white* ____ ____ *skin* ____ ____ *pink* An onset may consist of one or more ____________ letters. (vowel, consonant)
no consonant yes *ch*	**6.** There are many syllables and one-syllable words in the English language that do not begin with an onset. Examine the one-syllable word *at.* Does *at* begin with an onset? ____________ *At* does not begin with an onset because there is no ____________ letter preceding the vowel. Does the one-syllable word *chat* begin with an onset? ____________ The onset in the word *chat* is the consonant digraph ____________ .
off, it, add, out, up, elf	**7.** We have noted that a word or syllable may not always begin with an onset. Mark the one-syllable words below that do not begin with an onset. *off show it add out split up elf queen*

th t, p k, g d, m *ic*	**8.** Study the two-syllable words below. Write the onset that begins each syllable. *thir teen* *pump kin* *gar den* *mag ic* ___ ___ ___ ___ ___ ___ ___ ___ Which syllable in the words above does not begin with an onset? __________
consonant precedes *no*	**9.** We have learned that an onset is the __________ letter(s) that begins the syllable. We have also learned that an onset __________ (precedes, follows) the vowel in a syllable. Do we expect every syllable to begin with an onset? __________
rime vowel, consonant(s)	**10.** We call the vowel and the consonant(s) that follows it at the end of the syllable the __________ . *Rime* is a variation in the spelling of the word *rhyme.* The dictionary defines *rhyme* as "the agreement among the ending vowel and consonant sounds in words." Therefore, the rime consists of the __________ and the final __________ in a syllable.
spend, beg, strut *drink, stop, flat* one	**11.** Study the one-syllable words below. Underline the rime in each word. *spend* *beg* *strut* *drink* *stop* *flat* How many vowel phonemes do you hear in each one-syllable word? __________
2, 1, 2, 1, 3, 2 3, 3, 2, 1, 1, 3 rime	**12.** Use the number of the rime at the right to indicate the rime in the words below. 1. *ug* 2. *ant* 3. *op* *plant* ___ *bug* ___ *slant* ___ *dug* ___ *top* ___ *grant* ___ *drop* ___ *hop* ___ *chant* ___ *plug* ___ *rug* ___ *mop* ___ You can see that our written language has many words that have the same __________ .

Answer	Frame
en el, ase all, am age ump in one	**13.** Write the rime in each of the two-syllable words below. *ken nel* *base ball* *dam age* *pump kin* ___ ___ ___ ___ ___ ___ ___ ___ Each rime consists of ____________ vowel phoneme(s). (How many?)
can match kept tent ham salt trust	**14.** Study the rime in the words at the right to see if the rime always consists of one consonant which follows the vowel phoneme. Underline the rime in each one-syllable word. *can* *match* *kept* *tent* *ham* *salt* *trust*
consonant *lamp, swift, push, call, thought, sold*	**15.** We can see from the words in frame 14 that a rime may have more than one ____________ letter following the vowel phoneme. Mark the rimes in the one-syllable words below. *lamp* *swift* *push* *call* *thought* *sold*
amb one, silent	**16.** The rime in the one-syllable word *lamb* is ____________ . This rime consists of one vowel, *a,* and two consonant letters, *m* and *b.* Say *lamb* out loud. How many consonant phonemes do you hear in this rime? ____________ The last consonant letter is ____________ .
look sleep mouse write blame no train yes ride	**17.** Study the rimes in the words at the right. Underline the rime in each one-syllable word. *look* *sleep* *mouse* *write* *blame* *train* *ride* Does the rime always consist of one vowel letter? _____ Does each rime consist of one vowel phoneme? _____

sure *dance* *store* *home* *leave* *mouse*	**18.** Underline the rime in each word at the right. Now pronounce the words aloud. Notice that you hear only one vowel phoneme. *sure* *dance* *store* *home* *leave* *mouse*
rime consonant *ore, our, ent, aste;* *ain, ar, arve, oint*	**19.** We have noted that there is one ____________ in each syllable. The rime consists of the vowel and the ____________ letter(s) at the end of the syllable. Write the rime in each one-syllable word below. Work carefully. (If you correctly identify all the rimes, you are really thinking!) *more* *our* *cent* *taste* *rain* *star* *starve* *point* _____ _____ _____ _____ _____ _____ _____ _____
kīnd *băth* *sĭt* *tōld* *wĭn* *fĕd* *līght* *tŭb* CVC	**20.** Study the words at the right. Mark the vowel with a breve to indicate a short sound, and a macron to indicate a long sound. *kind* *bath* *sit* *told* *win* *fed* *light* *tub* These words consist of a ____________ vowel-consonant pattern. (CVC, CV)
short *ind, old, ight* long (glided)	**21.** We expect the vowel in the CVC vowel-consonant pattern to represent its ____________ sound. Write each rime in frame 20 that does not follow the CVC generalization ____________ . The vowel sound in the rimes that are exceptions to the CVC pattern represents a ____________ (long, short) sound. The CVC pattern does not give us clues to the pronunciation of the rimes *ind, old,* and *ight.*

	22. Mark the rime in each pair of words below.
bolt, colt, wild, child	*bolt* *wild* *scold* *high*
scold, told, high, sigh	*colt* *child* *told* *sigh*
	When you see a word you do not recognize, you can use your knowledge of the sounds which the onset and the rime represent to help you pronounce the word.
	23. Pronounce the groups of words below aloud.
	find *damp* *sight* *bug* *clear*
	blind *ramp* *light* *dug* *fear*
	kind *clamp* *flight* *hug* *dear*
	mind *stamp* *tight* *plug* *gear*
yes	Does each group of words have the same rime? ____________ Do
yes	the words in each group rhyme? ____________
	24. We have noted that when words have the same rime, the words
rhyme	may also _____ , as in *bug* and *dug.* There are exceptions (of course!), as we see in *cough* and *bough.*
	25. Now pronounce the sets of words below to see if the words that rhyme also contain the same rime. Mark the sets of words that have the same rime.
fish, wish	*fish* *joke* *pail* *deed*
deed, feed	*wish* *oak* *stale* *feed*
yes	Does each set of words rhyme? ____________ Does each set of
no	words have the same rime? ____________
rhymes	**26.** Each set of words in frame 25 ____________ . That is, in each set there is agreement among the ending vowel and the consonant
phonemes	sounds. We have learned that the same ____________ may be represented by different graphemes. Therefore, words which rhyme
rime	may not always consist of the same ____________ .

two one	**27.** There are many rimes in written English that have more than one vowel letter. Say the one-syllable words below aloud. *boat* *made* *store* *seed* The rimes in the words above consist of ________ vowel letters. (How many?) How many vowel phonemes do you hear in each rime? ________
vowel phoneme rime	**28.** We have seen that the rime consists of one ________ phoneme and the consonant(s) that follows the vowel phoneme in the syllable. We have learned that each syllable contains one vowel ________ . Therefore, each syllable must contain one and only one ________ . (onset, rime)
two two	**29.** Say the two-syllable words below aloud. *ti ger* *pic nic* *in tense* *blan ket* How many vowel sounds do you hear in each word? ________ Each word has ________ rimes.
two syllables rimes	**30.** If you hear two vowel phonemes in a word, you can be sure that the word has ________ rimes. You can also be sure that a word (How many?) with two rimes has two ________ . Therefore, the number of ________ in a word is equal to the number of syllables in a word.

r *ight* *s* *ave* *s* *at* *h* *urt* *d* *ish* *f* *ind* *b* *ig* *gr* *een*	**31.** Pronounce the one-syllable words at the right. Complete the table by filling in the onset (1), and the rime (2) for each word (3).	1 2 3 _____ _____ *right* _____ _____ *save* _____ _____ *sat* _____ _____ *hurt* _____ _____ *dish* _____ _____ *find* _____ _____ *big* _____ _____ *green*
consonant(s) vowel, consonant(s) onset rime vowel consonant	**32.** Let us review. We have learned that the onset is the _____________ at the beginning of the syllable (*b*oat), and the rime is the _____________ and _____________ that follows it at the end of the syllable (b*oat*). A word or a syllable may not have an _____________ (*oat*). However, the syllable must have a _____________ . The rime has one _____________ phoneme, and may have more than one _____________ letter(s) that follows the vowel (*dish*).	
scratch *bird* *street* *am* *twig* *shrine* *chick*	**33.** Now use your knowledge to combine the onset (1) with the rime (2) and write the one-syllable word (3) on the line at the right.	1 + 2 = 3 *scr* + *atch* = _____ *b* + *ird* = _____ *str* + *eet* = _____ + *am* = _____ *tw* + *ig* = _____ *shr* + *ine* = _____ *ch* + *ick* = _____

BOX 6.1

Onset and Rime, and 50 Common Rimes

Study Guide

Onset

The onset is the consonant that precedes the vowel in a syllable. The onset may have one (*cat*), two (*chat*), or three (*string*) consonant letters.

Rime

The rime consists of a vowel and the final consonant(s) in the syllable. The rime may have more than one vowel letter, but only one vowel phoneme (*reach*).

Rhyme

Rhyme is the agreement among the ending vowel and consonant phonemes in words (*rain, train* or *head, bed*). Words that share a rime (*rain, train*) may rhyme. Words that rhyme may not always share the same rime (*head, bed*). Furthermore, words that share the same rime may not always share the same ending vowel and consonant sounds (*head, bead*).

50 Common Rimes

Rime	Examples	Rime	Examples
ab	*cab, grab, lab, tab*	*ell*	*bell, fell, sell, tell*
ace	*face, place, race, space*	*en*	*den, hen, men, pen*
ack	*back, black, sack, track*	*ent*	*bent, sent, tent, went*
ad	*bad, had, mad, sad*	*est*	*best, rest, test, west*
ade	*grade, made, shade, trade*	*et*	*bet, set, pet, wet*
ag	*bag, flag, rag, tag*	*ice*	*dice, mice, nice, twice*
ail	*fail, mail, sail, tail*	*ick*	*brick, lick, quick, trick*
ain	*gain, main, pain, train*	*ide*	*bride, side, tide, wide*
air	*chair, fair, pair, stair*	*ig*	*big, dig, pig, wig*
ake	*bake, make, take, wake*	*ight*	*fight, night, right, sight*
all	*ball, call, fall, tall*	*ill*	*bill, fill, hill, pill*
am	*clam, ham, ram, slam*	*in*	*fin, pin, thin, win*
ame	*came, game, name, same*	*ing*	*king, ring, sing, sting*
amp	*camp, damp, lamp, stamp*	*ink*	*link, pink, sink, wink*
an	*can, fan, man, tan*	*ip*	*dip, hip, ship, slip*
and	*band, hand, land, sand*	*it*	*hit, pit, sit, slit*
ang	*bang, hang, rang, sang*	*ock*	*block, rock, sock, stock*
ank	*blank, drank, rank, sank*	*og*	*dog, frog, hog, log*
ap	*cap, lap, map, nap*	*old*	*cold, fold, hold, told*
at	*cat, fat, hat, sat*	*op*	*hop, mop, pop, stop*
ate	*date, gate, late, rate*	*ot*	*dot, hot, got, lot*
eam	*beam, cream, dream, team*	*ug*	*bug, dug, hug, tug*
eat	*beat, meat, neat, seat*	*ump*	*bump, dump, hump, pump*
ed	*bed, fed, led, red*	*un*	*bun, fun, run, sun*
eed	*deed, feed, need, seed*	*ut*	*but, cut, nut, shut*

Review 23

1. Write the onset for each of the one-syllable words below.

   wrong *could* *shop* *high* *stay*
   sun *bowl* *school* *stage* *goat*

2. Which of the one-syllable words below do <u>not</u> begin with an onset?

   ask *loss* *fan* *ouch* *am*
   blue *green* *leave* *old* *if*

3. The rime consists of one ______________ phoneme and the ______________ which follows in the syllable.

4. Write the rime for each of the one-syllable words below.

   strain *sent* *mice* *swamp* *flour*
   child *bought* *since* *house* *trip*

5. Which of the one-syllable words above have rimes which include more than one vowel letter?

   (See the Answers section for the answers to Review 23.)

Recap III

26 consonants phonemes	1. Phonics is the study of the relationship of letters and letter combinations to the sounds they represent. There are _____ letters in our alphabet, classified as vowels and ______________ . These letters and combinations represent the 44 sounds, or ______________ , used in the American-English language. (This is oversimplified, but adequate in this step of the process of teaching children to read.)
phoneme phoneme 44 phonemes	2. How easy the development of independence in decoding would be if each letter represented one and only one ______________ , and each phoneme was represented by only one letter! You know that is not the case; however, you have gained an understanding of the patterns within the inconsistencies. You have also developed a one-to-one correspondence between grapheme and ______________ by selecting a key symbol to represent each of the _____ ______________ of the language.

pronunciation phoneme accented accented vowel vowel *i (ĭ), ə (schwa)*	**3.** Another relationship is that of the syllable to the word. A syllable is a unit of ____________ . Each syllable must have one and only one vowel ____________ . Each word has one syllable which receives the greatest amount of stress. We call this the ____________ syllable. If a word has only one syllable, that is the ____________ syllable. There is a strong relationship between the ____________ (vowel, consonant) and the accented syllable. The ____________ in the unaccented syllable often is represented by the soft, short sound of ____ or by the ___________ .
syllables accented	**4.** You have become acquainted with the clues that help you (1) to divide a word into ____________ , and (2) to determine which syllable is ____________ . The following frames present specific words, selected to illustrate your knowledge of the syllable-accent generalizations as well as to review other learnings.
see-saw, see′ saw (sē′ sô) compound first, compound	**5.** On the blanks after each word (1) rewrite it as an entry word in the dictionary (useful for end-of-the-line hyphenation); (2) rewrite, adding the accent; and (3) in parenthesis, using all your knowledge of phonemes, rewrite the word showing pronunciation. To make this study more effective, as you work, say the generalizations of syllables, accents, and other understandings to yourself. Also fill in the other blanks as indicated. *seesaw* ____________ ____________ ____________ Using the word *seesaw* as an example, say to yourself, "*Seesaw* is a ____________ word; the syllabic division comes between the words of which it is composed." (Fill in the first blank.) "The accent usually falls on or within the ____________ word of a ____________ word." (Fill in blank two.) On blank three, mark the word for pronunciation.

s two one long silent ē ô *ball* *(sē′sô)*	**6.** Continue your conversation about *seesaw:* "We represent the consonant phonemes in *seesaw* with _____ . The first syllable has ______________ vowel letters. We know that each syllable can have only ______________ vowel phoneme. When there are two vowel letters in a syllable, generally the first is ______________ and the second is ______________ . So the phoneme in the first syllable is represented by _____ . In the second 'word' the vowel phoneme is *w*-controlled. The key symbol is ______________ ; the key word is ______________ ." (But maybe you prefer to use *ought* (*ôt*) as the key word. Do you?) The third blank, frame 5, reads ______________ . Examine the footnote. Turn to page 210. Read items 4 and 9. Did you use them in your conversation? How about S1 and A2 on page 211? V 4, V 9, S 1, A 2*
s, i *cit-rus, cit′ rus* *(sĭt′ r əs)*	**7.** The second word in your study is *citrus.* (Caution: Although you can achieve correct results immediately, don't do it that way. This is your opportunity to review by yourself your understandings of the generalizations, syllables, accents, etc., including "*c* usually represents the _____ phoneme when followed by _____ .") Selected references to the Appendix* are given. Check your "conversation" after each frame. Did you include these generalizations? Also note irregularities in consonant and vowel phonemes. *citrus* ______________ ______________ ______________ C 2, V 6, V 15, S 5, A 4*
un but ton ing *un but′ ton ing* *(ŭn bŭt′ ən ĭng) or* *(ən bŭt′ ən ĭŋ)*	**8.** Continue with the words as given in each of the following frames. *unbuttoning* ______________ ______________ ______________ V 6, V 15, S 2, S 5, A 1, A 4*

*Key to generalizations (Appendix): C: Consonant, p. 209; V: Vowel, p. 210; S: Syllable, p. 211; A: Accent, p. 211.

ad mi ra tion *ad mi ra'tion* *(ăd mə rā' shən)*	**9.** *admiration* ________ ________ ________ S 2, A 5*
wrin kle wring' kle *(ring' kəl)*	**10.** *wrinkle* ________ ________ ________ C 1a.n, S 3, A 7*
1. *an nex an nex'* *(ə nĕks')* 2. *an nex an' nex* *(ăn' ĕks)*	1. 2. **11.** We will *annex* the land on which the new *annex* was built. 1. ________ ________ ________ 2. ________ ________ ________ A 3*
ti ger ti' ger *(tī' gər)*	**12.** *tiger* ________ ________ ________ S 4*
weath er weath'er *(wĕth' ər)*	**13.** *weather* ________ ________ ________ S 6*
con tain con tain' *(kən tān')*	**14.** *contain* ________ ________ ________ C 2, V 10, A 6*

*Key to generalizations (Appendix): C: Consonant, p. 209; V: Vowel, p. 210; S: Syllable, p. 211; A: Accent, p. 211.

on ion on′ion *(ŭn′ yən)* consonant	**15.** *onion* ________ ________ ________ Is this *y* a vowel or a consonant? ________ C 6, S 5, A 4*
reading (Children should know the words at the hearing level.)	**16.** Turn to the Appendix. Restudy the generalizations to check your thinking. I hope you are saying, "I did very well." ("perfect"—?) The problem we face is that you know these words. If you were attacking words not in your ________ (reading, listening) vocabulary, you would have a better test of your phonics ability.
onset, rime consonant phoneme follows	**17.** Another way to analyze the syllable is to divide it into the ________ and the ________ . You know that the onset is the ________ letter(s) that begins the syllable, and the rime is the vowel ________ and the consonant letter(s) that ________ the vowel phoneme.
pen *cil* *p* *en* *c* *il*	**18.** Using your knowledge of the onset and the rime in the syllable, divide the word *pencil* into syllables. Then analyze the two syllables into onsets and rimes. The word *pencil* consists of the two syllables ________ and ________ . The first syllable, *pen,* consists of the onset ________ and the rime ________ . The second syllable, *cil,* consists of the onset ________ and the rime ________ .

*Key to generalizations (Appendix): C: Consonant, p. 209; V: Vowel, p. 210; S: Syllable, p. 211; A: Accent, p. 211.

	19. Now continue to identify the onset and the rime in each of the syllables you identify in the following words.
sur	The word *surprise* consists of two syllables ______________ and
prise	______________ .
s, ur	The first syllable, *sur,* consists of the onset _____ and the rime _______ .
pr	The second syllable, *prise,* consists of the onset _____ and the rime
ise	_____ .
lav	The word *lavender* consists of the three syllables ______________ ,
en, der	_____ and _____ .
l	The first syllable, *lav,* consists of the onset ______________ and the
av	rime _____ .
en	The second syllable, *en,* consists of the rime _____ .
d, er	The third syllable, *der,* consists of the onset _____ and the rime _____ .
	20. You have studied the relationship of letters and letter
sounds (phonemes)	combinations to the ______________ they represent and have built a
phonics	depth of understanding in the content of ______________ . You will use that content to help those learning to read to develop skill in the recognition and identification of words. It must be pointed out that the use of phonics is the basis of <u>one</u> of the word-attack skills (skills needed to attain independence in reading) and that the mastery of
reading	the total ______________ process requires the development of still other sets of skills, including the understanding of the material read. Reading is a complicated process!
	21. You are now ready for the posttest. Show your mastery of the content of phonics! Best wishes.

Self-evaluation II:

A Posttest

This test is designed to help you evaluate your growth in the field of phonics. Read each item, including all choices. Indicate the answer you consider best by circling the appropriate letter (a, b, c, d, or e) or by marking the appropriate letter on an answer sheet. Please respond to every item. Time: 30 minutes.

I. Multiple Choice. Select the best answer.

1. Which of the following most adequately completes the sentence? The consonant phonemes in the English language are represented by

- **a.** the consonant-vowel combinations.
- **b.** the distinctive speech sounds we associate with each of the 21 consonant letters of the alphabet.
- **c.** 18 of the consonant letters of the alphabet plus seven digraphs.
- **d.** the single-letter consonants plus their two- and three-letter blends.
- **e.** the English language is too irregular to represent the consonant phonemes with any degree of accuracy.

2. The second syllable of the nonsense word *omethbin* would be expected to rhyme with

a. see. **b.** pet. **c.** wreath. **d.** breath. **e.** kin.

3. The open syllable in the nonsense word *phattoe* would be expected to rhyme with

a. *fa* of fatal. **b.** day. **c.** fat. **d.** dough. **e.** a and b.

4. How many phonemes are represented in the nonsense word *ghight?*

a. one **b.** two **c.** three **d.** four **e.** six

5. The sound of the *schwa* is represented by

- **a.** the *a* in *carry.*
- **b.** the *e* in *lemon.*
- **c.** the *i* in *lighted.*
- **d.** the *o* in *falcon.*
- **e.** the *u* in *rule.*

6. A diphthong is best illustrated by the vowels representing the sound of
   a. *oo* in *foot.*
   b. *oy* in *employ.*
   c. *ow* in *low.*
   d. *ai* in *said.*
   e. All of the above.
7. Generally, when two like-consonants appear together in a word
   a. one is sounded with the first syllable and the other with the second.
   b. both are sounded when the preceding vowel is *e.*
   c. both are sounded when the following vowel is *i.*
   d. only one is sounded.
   e. neither is sounded.
8. A requirement of a syllable is that
   a. it contain no more than one vowel letter.
   b. it contain no more than one vowel phoneme.
   c. it contain at least one consonant phoneme.
   d. it contain no more than one phoneme.
   e. None of the above.
9. An example of a closed syllable is found in the word
   a. *low.*
   b. *sofa.*
   c. *doubt.*
   d. All of these.
   e. None of these.
10. The letter *y* is most likely to be a consonant when
    a. it follows *o* in a syllable.
    b. it has the sound of *i* as in *light.*
    c. it is the first letter in a word or syllable.
    d. it is the last letter in a word or syllable.
    e. None of the above.
11. The letter *q* could be removed from the alphabet because it could adequately and without conflict be represented by
    a. *ch* as in *chair.*
    b. *k* as in *kite.*
    c. *cu* as in *cubic.*
    d. All of the above.
    e. The idea is foolish; *qu* represents a distinctive consonant phoneme.

12. An example of an open syllable is found in the word

a. *be.*
b. *replay.*
c. *tree.*
d. All of these.
e. None of these.

13. Which of the following has the incorrect diacritical mark?

a. băll **b.** fĕll **c.** wĭsh **d.** drŏp **e.** cŭt

14. Which of the following has an incorrect diacritical mark?

a. spāde **b.** rēady **c.** insīde **d.** lōne **e.** fūse

15. When *o* and *a* appear together in a syllable, they usually represent the same sound as

a. the *a* in *bacon.*
b. the *o* in *done.*
c. the *o* in *force.*
d. the *o* in *ghostly.*
e. the *a* in *camel.*

16. The symbol *s* is used in the dictionary to show the pronunciation of the sound heard in

a. *should.* **b.** *has.* **c.** *sure.* **d.** *zoo.* **e.** *waltz.*

17. If *e* were the only vowel in an open syllable, that *e* would most likely represent the same sound as

a. the *y* in *by.*
b. the *ea* in *seat.*
c. the *e* in *get.*
d. the *e* in *fine.*
e. None of these.

18. The consonant cluster is illustrated by

a. the *ch* in *chin.*
b. the *ng* in *sing.*
c. the *bl* in *black.*
d. the *ph* in *graph.*
e. a, c, and d.

19. When the single vowel *i* in an accented syllable is followed by a single consonant and a final *e,* the *i* would most likely have the sound of

a. the *i* in *readily.*
b. the *i* in *active.*
c. the *y* in *cry.*
d. the *e* in *sea.*
e. the *y* in *happy.*

20. If *a* were the single vowel in an accented syllable ending with a consonant, that *a* would most likely represent the same sound as

a. the *ay* in *daylight.*
b. the *a* in *mad.*
c. the *a* in *many.*
d. the *a* in *wall.*
e. the *a* in *car.*

21. When *c* is followed by *i*, it is most likely to represent the same sound as

a. the *c* in *cube.*
b. the *c* in *chime.*
c. the *c* in *cello.*
d. *c* followed by *o.*
e. None of these.

22. The word *if* ends with the same sound as

a. the *ph* of *phrase.*
b. the *f* in *of.*
c. the *gh* in *cough.*
d. All of the above.
e. a and c.

23. The symbol *w* is used in the dictionary to show the pronunciation of the sound heard in

a. *want.* **b.** *now.* **c.** *who.* **d.** *two.* **e.** a, b, and c.

24. When the letter *g* is followed by *a,* it most likely will represent the same sound as

a. the *j* in *jam.*
b. the *g* in *go.*
c. the *g* in *gnat.*
d. the *g* in *bring.*
e. the *g* in *giant.*

II. Complete each sentence by selecting the word for which the correct pronunciation is indicated.

25. When I picked my vegetables, I dropped a

a. *răd′ ĭsh.* **b.** *kăr′ŏt.* **c.** *kŭ kŭm′ bĕr.* **d.** *pë.* **e.** *kăb′ ĭg.*

26. I went to the park for a

a. *kŏn′ cûrt.* **b.** *rās.* **c.** *wôlk.* **d.** *pĭk′ nək.* **e.** *păr′ tē.*

27. The wall is

a. *t̸hĭn.* **b.** *stŭck′ o͝od.* **c.** *pĭngk.* **d.** *lōu.* **e.** *krăk′əd.*

28. The tree we planted was a

a. *fĭr.* **b.** *ăzh.* **c.** *spro͞os.* **d.** *bərtch.* **e.** *cē kwoi′ə.*

29. I went to the grocery store for

a. *ôr'ĭng əz.* **b.** *brēd.* **c.** *jăm.* **d.** *ko͞ok'ēz.* **e.** *kăn'dȳ.*

30. I washed the

a. *wôls.* **b.** *wĭnd'ōs.* **c.** *kown'tər.* **d.** *nīvz.* **e.** *sĭnk.*

III. Multiple Choice. Where does the accent fall in the words or nonsense words given at the left? Indicate your answer by selecting the last two letters of the accented syllable found in the same row as the word.

Look at the example: *showboat.* The first "word" in a compound word is generally accented: *show'boat.* Look for the last two letters of *show, ow,* in the row to the right.

You would circle b or mark b on your answer sheet.

Example:

showboat	**a.** ho	(**b.**) ow	**c.** bo	**d.** at	
31. tenlaim	**a.** te	**b.** en	**c.** nl	**d.** la	**e.** im
32. grottome	**a.** ro	**b.** ot	**c.** to	**d.** om	**e.** me
33. religherly	**a.** re	**b.** nl	**c.** gh	**d.** er	**e.** ly
34. pnight	**a.** pn	**b.** ni	**c.** ig	**d.** gh	**e.** ht
35. damapantion	**a.** am	**b.** ma	**c.** pa	**d.** an	**e.** on
36. present (verb)	**a.** re	**b.** es	**c.** se	**d.** nt	**e.** pr

IV. Multiple Choice. Select the word in each row which is incorrectly syllabicated.

37.	**a.** li ly	**b.** li lac	**c.** fa tal	**d.** ma trix	**e.** lu rid
38.	**a.** fin ger	**b.** cot ton	**c.** gamb ol	**d.** for get	**e.** pas tel
39.	**a.** par don a ble	**b.** re sist i ble	**c.** in dent ion	**d.** in fu sion	**e.** ex hale
40.	**a.** saw dust	**b.** to get her	**c.** side walk	**d.** shark skin	**e.** loop hole

V. Multiple Choice. There are three words in each item (a, b, c). Select the word in which you would hear the same sound as that represented by the underlined part of the word at the left. You may find that the sound is heard in all three words; if so, mark d. If none of the words contain the sound, mark e.

41. tent	**a.** missed	**b.** listen	**c.** catch	**d.** All	**e.** None
42. pleasure	**a.** vision	**b.** sabotage	**c.** rouge	**d.** All	**e.** None
43. tanker	**a.** banner	**b.** singer	**c.** nose	**d.** All	**e.** None
44. gem	**a.** edge	**b.** soldier	**c.** jelly	**d.** All	**e.** None
45. that	**a.** bath	**b.** theory	**c.** this	**d.** All	**e.** None
46. chill	**a.** chute	**b.** chord	**c.** question	**d.** All	**e.** None
47. hook	**a.** pool	**b.** moose	**c.** tooth	**d.** All	**e.** None
48. ace	**a.** bead	**b.** said	**c.** lab	**d.** All	**e.** None

49. now a. snow b. joyous c. cow d. All e. None
50. sock a. sure b. sugar c. city d. All e. None

VI. Multiple Choice. Select the letter(s) at the right that represents the onset in the one-syllable words.

51. might a. mi b. ight c. m d. migh e. igh
52. scratch a. scr b. ch c. sc d. scra e. atch
53. choice a. oi b. ce c. oice d. ch e. choi
54. ghost a. st b. gh c. hos d. ost e. gho
55. blank a. ank b. la c. lan d. bla e. bl

VII. Multiple Choice. Select the letter(s) at the right that represents the rime in the one-syllable words.

56. climb a. cl b. imb c. mb d. limb e. cli
57. juice a. ui b. jui c. ce d. uice e. j
58. shoal a. oal b. oa c. hoa d. sh e. al
59. spill a. ll b. sp c. pill d. spi e. ill
60. prince a. nce b. rince c. ince d. ce e. pr

(See p. 203 for answers to Self-evaluation II.)

Self-evaluation II: Number correct _____

Self-evaluation I: Number correct _____

Answers to the Reviews

These reviews give you an indication of your mastery (or lack of mastery) of the material. WORK TO ACHIEVE 100% ON EACH REVIEW! Your success depends largely on your self-motivation. It takes very little more effort to achieve mastery than to fail, even while writing each answer. The difference depends on your mind-set. Reread the section INTRODUCTION. Good luck!

Review 1

1. decode **2.** phoneme **3.** 44 **4.** /*m*/ **5.** allophones
6. segment (or separate), blend **7.** segmenting **8.** blending
9. grapheme **10.** no **11.** graphophonic **12.** syntactic
13. semantic

Scores:

Review 2

1. no **2.** phonemes (The key symbols represent sounds, never letters.)
3. *m* **4.** *m* **5.** 2, digraphs **6.** letters **7.** digraph, one

Scores:

Review 3

1. 5, 5 **2.** 3, 3 **3.** digraphs **4.** *c, q, x* They are represented by other letters; they have no distinctive phonemes of their own. **5.** key symbols, key words **6.** *m, k, r, v* **7.** *u,* silent, *w* **8.** *m v r, k w v r*
9. When we see a *v* in a word, we know it represents the same sound as that heard at the beginning of *van.*

Scores:

Review 4

1. a. no **b.** *saf* **c.** *mel* **d.** *plara* **e.** *gaeve* **f.** *lam* **g.** *kak* **h.** *tovom* **i.** *rok* **j.** *rim* **k.** *kwimel* **l.** *klopem* **m.** *voter* **2.** digraphs, one, no (*kl* represents two phonemes.) **3.** We are apt to add a vowel sound. **4.** The key symbols represent the sounds of our language. Each sound is represented once. *Q* would be a duplication.

Scores:

If you have missed any items in previous reviews, take that review now. Write the second score following the first. Does it show improvement?

Review 5

1. a. *b* **b.** *t f* **c.** *h j* **d.** *v* **e.** *f n* **f.** *t t* **g.** *g s t l* **h.** *s l j r* **i.** *j n d r* **j.** *h f t* **k.** *p l n t d* **l.** *k w l t* **m.** *z r* **n.** *s l* **o.** *k l m* **2. a.** *don't, ride, moved* **b.** *fine, graph, photo, off* **c.** *wedge, soldier, Roger* **d.** *knot, stranger* **e.** *his, puzzle, does*

Scores:

If you missed any, turn to the appropriate pages and restudy. Select a previous review. Write the answers. Did you better your score or maintain a perfect score? Be sure you write your scores for each review and "review of reviews."

Review 6

1. A *g* followed by *e, i,* or *y* generally has the sound of /*j*/; a *g* followed by *a, o, u,* any consonant, or at the end of a word is /*g*/ as in goat. **2. a.** *j n t* **b.** *b ng k* **c.** *g r l* **d.** *b g* **e.** *m sh n* **f.** *k k* **g.** *h* **h.** *m ch* **i.** *y l* **j.** *w* **k.** *k w k* **l.** *r t* **m.** *y* t **n.** *n k* **3.** *girl* **4.** *C* followed by *e, i,* or *y* generally has the sound of /*s*/; *c* followed by *a, o, u,* any consonant, or at the end of a word is /*k*/ **5.** *ed, d, t* **6.** The consonants *w* (as in *we,* /*w*/) and *y* (as in yes, /*y*/) appear before the vowel in a syllable. **7. a.** *g* **b.** *ch* **c.** *j* **d.** *k* **e.** *j* **f.** *k* **g.** *k* **h.** *k* **i.** *k* **j.** *f* **8.** digraphs **9.** *ranje, ring*kle, ransom; manjer, trianggle, lingks **10.** *e, i, y* **11.** digraph, *go, j,* silent

Scores:

There were some tricky words in this review. Sincere congratulations if you had them all correct. If you did not, make sure you understand the principle involved. Restudy the appropriate section. Plan to "review this review" soon.

Review 7

1. a. *e,i,y* *k* *a,o,u* **b.** *k* **c.** *ks,gz,z* **2. a.** hard *a,o,u* **b.** soft *j* *e,i,y* **3. a.** some **b.** *z* **4.** *d* *t* **5.** *v* **6.** *ch* *sh* **7. a.** *s, sh, z, zh;* *z, s, zh* **b.** *c, z;* *z, s, x* (any two) **c.** *k,g,h* silent; *t* silent **8. a.** graphemes, phoneme **b.** phonemes, grapheme **c.** phoneme

Scores:

Review 8

1. digraph **2.** *k* *k, h, zh, wh* *th; wh* *ch, th, w* *th, sh; sh* *g, w* *sh, v* *zh, ng* **3.** *weather, which, belong, wish, both, through* (If you omitted the *wh* of *which,* you are correct also.) **4.** letter, 7, digraphs, *sh, ch, wh, zh, th, th, ng* **5.** *gh* in *tough, ch* in *chloroform, ph* in *phoneme* **6.** *f, k, f* **7.** *sungk, fotograf, now* (*no*), *alfabet, feazant, kouf*

Scores:

Continue those reviews of reviews so as to improve scores or maintain perfect scores!

Review 9

1. a. *sh* *v* *r* **b.** *gz* **c.** *sh* *r* **d.** *sh* *r* **e.** *t* *r* *zh* *r* **f.** *k* *r* *k* *t* *r* **g.** *b* *r* *zh* *r* **h.** *k* *r* *s* *m* *s* **i.** *s* *k* *l* *z* **j.** *g* *s* *t* *s* **k.** *ch* *r* *j* **l.** *sh* *t* **m.** *k* *w* *k* **n.** *l* *sh* *n* **o.** *d* *v* *zh* *n* **p.** *sh* *k* *g* **q.** *s* *t* *r* *ng* **2.** The digraph does not appear in a word.

Scores:

Review 10

1. *ng (swing), wh (white), zh (measure), th(mother), sh (flash), ch (porch)* **2.** *breath* **3.** (1)—(*l* is silent), (2) *yo-yo,* (3) *sun,* (4) *table,* (5) *jeep,* (6)—(7)—(8)—(9) *van,* (10) *goat,* (11)—(12)—(13)—(not a consonant), (14) *ring,* (15) *lion,* (16) *ring* **4.** is not, does not **5.** consonant **6.** *this* *father* *feather* *them* **7.** *wheel* *white* *whip* *whistle* **8.** Each appears at the beginning of a word or syllable and has a vowel following.

Scores:

Review 11

1. *ng* **2. a.** *mang go, man jer, man jy* (The following are spaced only to make them more distinct, not to indicate syllables.) If you get these, you're good! **b.** *pin, pi ng, pi ng k, pi ng-po ng* **c.** *ban, ba ng, ba ng k, ba ng k i ng* **d.** *ran, ra ng, ra ng k, ra ng k i ng* **e.** *ran ch er, ran je, fan sy* **3. a.** *b, d, f, g, h, j, k, l, m, n, p, r, s, t, v, w, y, z* **b.** digraphs *sh, ch, wh, zh, th, th, ng* **4.** *C* has no distinctive sound of its own. It is represented by the *s* and *k*. **5.** *q, x* **6.** *Ph* is represented by *f.* **7.** *hole, hi, kwik, gofer, holy, fone, thach, that, taut, kom, glisening, dauter, rusle, dout, not, bujet, rap, thingking*

Scores:

Review 12

1. You hear the sounds represented by the letters in the cluster; a digraph represents a new sound. **2.** The blends are represented by phonemes we already know. **3.** *zh (pleasure) th(the) ng (nearing) th (through) ch (changed) wh (wheel) sh (shoulder)* **4.** *egzit* or *eksit, kuickly (kwikly), sity* **5.** */st/, /pl/, /tr/, /dr/, /thr/, /kw/, /sl/.*

Scores:

This is a good time to take stock of the reviews. Is there material you need to study? Do it now.

Review 13

1. *a, e, i, o, u, w, y* **2.** *w, y* **3.** C, V, V, C, V, C **4.** consonant digraph **5.** more **6.** 19

Scores:

Review 14

1. a. When there is a single vowel in a closed accented syllable, that vowel phoneme is usually short. **b.** When a word or a syllable has two vowels, one of which is a final *e,* and the two vowels are separated by two consonants, the first vowel usually represents the short sound and the final *e* is silent. **2.** *bĕd, nĕxt, lŏt, căt, trĭp, skĭn, mŏp, ŭs, sĕnd, bŭg.* **3.** VC, CVC, CVCCe (or VCCe), CVC, VC, CVCCe (or VCCe). **4.** *e, i, y*

Scores:

Review 15

1. *ē, ī, ō, ū* macron **2.** *i, e* **3.** *e* When a vowel or accented syllable has two vowels, one of which is the final *e,* the *e* is silent and the first vowel usually represents its long (glided) sound. **4.** accented, long **5.** end, long **6.** sound (or phoneme) **7.** d*in*e C n, tack, C k, way V a, watch, C ch, table C l, hello V o, tight C t, enough C f **8.** bīte, bĭt, căn, cāne, pĕt, Pēte, ŭs, fūse, cŏt, cōde.

Scores:

Review 16

1. *schwa* **2.** It saves assigning separate diacritical marks to each vowel to indicate a phoneme all share. **3.** *river* **4.** *regal, handmade* or *handmaid, celebrate, episode*

Scores:

Review 17

1. short or unglided, *ă, ĕ, ĭ, ŏ, ŭ* **2.** long or glided, *ā, ē, ī, ō, ū* **3.** *schwa,* ə, *agree* (ə *gre*) It saves assigning separate diacritical marks to each vowel to indicate a phoneme all share. **4.** following *r, l,* and *w* **5. a.** *ball* (*bôl*) **b.** *fur* (*fûr*) **c.** *father* (fäthər) **d.** *care* (*kâr*)

Scores:

(How did you do? You can feel a *real* sense of accomplishment if you had all of these correct. They are not easy!)

Review 18

1. *oi, ou* **2.** vowel **3.** *owl-ou, cow-ou, moist-oi, oyster-oi* **4.** *hous boi ouns ĕnjoi noiz brou*

Scores:

Review 19

1. A digraph is a two-letter grapheme which represents a single phoneme. **2.** o͞o, o͝o **3.** You cannot tell. The only clue is that it is most often o͞o as in *food.* **4.** *to͞oth, spo͞on, book, lo͞os, stood, mo͞o, shook* **5.** *klo͞od* **6.** *bo͞ot, fŭdj, doun, toi, shook, kō kō, nīt, fro͞ot, thrō, thro͞o, thō, thôt, kwĭt, book, smo͞oth, fo͞ol, brĕth, brēth, nīt*

Scores:

Review 20

1. diphthong, *oi, ou, house;* digraph, o͞o, o͝o in *hook.* **2.** When two vowels appear together in a word or syllable, the first usually represents the long sound and the second is silent. **3.** When a one-syllable word has an ending pattern CVCe, the first vowel is generally long and the *e* is silent. **4.** letter, phoneme

Scores:

Review 21

1. syllable **2.** phoneme **3.** yes **4.** no **5.** accented

6. a. The accent usually falls on or within the root word. *in ter change'a ble*

b. In compound words, the accent usually falls on the first word. *cow' boy*

c. One-syllable words are accented. *fast'* or *fast*

d. When a word functions as different parts of speech, the accent is usually on the first syllable of the noun. *ex'port* (noun)

e. The primary accent is usually on the syllable preceding the *tion* ending. *na' tion*

f. The accent usually falls on the syllable that closes with the first letter of a double consonant. *dol' lar*

g. When two vowel letters are within the last syllable of a two-syllable word, that last syllable is most often accented. *con ceal'*

h. When there is no other clue, the accent most often falls on the first syllable of a two-syllable word. *pa'per*

Scores:

Answers to Self-evaluation

I. Pretest

1. c	**13.** d	**25.** b	**37.** a	**49.** b
2. b	**14.** b	**26.** e	**38.** c	**50.** c
3. a	**15.** d	**27.** d	**39.** d	**51.** d
4. a	**16.** c	**28.** d	**40.** d	**52.** a
5. c	**17.** a	**29.** d	**41.** b	**53.** a
6. d	**18.** e	**30.** b	**42.** b	**54.** d
7. b	**19.** d	**31.** e	**43.** c	**55.** e
8. c	**20.** b	**32.** e	**44.** c	**56.** b
9. c	**21.** a	**33.** b	**45.** c	**57.** b
10. d	**22.** e	**34.** a	**46.** d	**58.** a
11. d	**23.** b	**35.** c	**47.** e	**59.** c
12. a	**24.** b	**36.** b	**48.** b	**60.** a

Review 22

1. a.	CV/CVCC	The syllable division is between the single vowel and the single consonant.
b.	CVC/CVC	The syllable division is between the two consonants when there is a single vowel on both sides of the two consonants.
c.	CVC/CV	The syllable division is between the two consonants when there is a single vowel on both sides of the two consonants.
d.	CCV/CVCC	The syllable division is between the single vowel and the single consonant.
2. a.	*re spect ful*	Suffixes and prefixes generally make separate syllables. This root word has one syllable.
b.	*ca pa ble*	The syllable division is between the single vowel and single consonant. If the last syllable of a word ends in *le* preceded by a consonant, that consonant usually begins the last syllable.
c.	*fa ther*	You cannot divide between letters of a digraph; treat the digraph as though it were one consonant. The division is between the single vowel and the digraph.

Scores:

Review 23

1. *wr, c, sh, h, st, s, b, sch, st, g* **2.** *ask, ouch, am, old, if* **3.** vowel, consonant(s) **4.** *ain, ent, ice, amp, our, ild, ought, ince, ouse, ip* **5.** *rain, flour, bought, since, house*

Scores:

Answers to Self-evaluation

II. Posttest

1. c
2. d
3. d
4. c
5. d
6. b
7. d
8. b
9. c
10. c
11. b
12. d
13. a
14. b
15. d
16. e
17. b
18. c
19. c
20. b
21. e
22. e
23. a
24. b
25. a
26. b
27. c
28. c
29. c
30. d
31. e
32. b
33. c
34. e
35. d
36. d
37. a
38. c
39. c
40. b
41. a
42. d
43. b
44. d
45. c
46. c
47. e
48. e
49. c
50. c
51. c
52. a
53. d
54. b
55. e
56. b
57. d
58. a
59. e
60. c

Glossary*

Accented syllable A syllable that receives greater stress than the other syllables in a word. *156*

Allophone A variant form of the same phoneme (as the /p/ in *pin* and the /p/ in *spin*). *12*

Blending The ability to combine individual phonemes together so as to pronounce a meaningful word (/m/ + /a/ + /n/ = /man/). *18*

Breve A diacritical mark (˘) used to indicate the short (unglided) sound of a vowel, as in the /ĕ/ in *red*. *99*

Closed syllable A syllable that ends in a consonant phoneme (*trip*). *103*

Compound word A word made up of two or more shorter words (*cowboy* and *rainbow*). *159*

Consonant One of the two classifications of speech sounds. To be precise in definition is more a function of phonetics than of phonics. Consonant sounds are "noisy," in that the speaker modifies or interrupts the stream of outgoing air (/p/, /s/, /j/). *25*

Consonant blend A combination of two or more adjacent consonant phonemes pronounced rapidly, as the */bl/* in *blue,* the */st/* in *still,* and the */spl/* in *splash.* The term refers to the sounds which the consonant clusters represent. *87*

Consonant cluster Two or more consonant letters appearing together in a syllable which, when sounded, form a consonant blend. Consonant clusters are taught as units rather than as single graphemes (e.g., *st* as representing two blended phonemes rather than an isolated /s/ and an isolated /t/. *87*

Consonant digraph Two-letter consonant combinations that represent phonemes not represented by the single letters, such as the *sh* in *shoe.* *72*

Decoding Translating graphemes into the sounds of spoken language so as to pronounce a visually unfamiliar word. Teachers may refer to this process of word identification as "sounding out" words. *9*

Digraph A grapheme composed of two letters which represent one speech sound (phoneme). *26, 136*

Diphthong A single vowel phoneme resembling a "glide" from one sound to another, represented by the graphemes *oi* (*/noise/*), *oy* (*/toy/*), *ou* (*/found/*), and *ow* (*now*): key symbols *oi* and *ou*; key words *oil* and *house.* *133*

*The number following each entry refers to the page on which the word is introduced.

Grapheme The written symbol used to represent the phoneme. It may be composed of one or more letters, and the same grapheme may represent more than one phoneme. *12*

Graphophonic cues The 26 letters (graphemes), the 44 sounds (phonemes), and the system of relationships among graphemes and phonemes. These cues are used to translate the written code into the sounds of spoken language. *19*

Key symbol Forty-four specific graphemes representing the 44 phonemes of the American-English language (as presented in this text), thus achieving a one-to-one correspondence between key symbol and phoneme: one symbol for each phoneme; one phoneme for each symbol. *29*

Key word One word selected for each of the 44 phonemes, identifying the specific phoneme. *30*

Long vowel The five vowels represented *a, e, i, o,* and *u* which, in the context of the teaching of phonics, are indicated by a macron (-) and "say their names." Key words: *apron, eraser, ice, overalls,* and *unicorn.* These vowels are also referred to as glided vowels. *108*

Macron A diacritical mark (-) used to indicate the long (glided) sound of a vowel. *108*

Onset One or more consonant letters which precede the vowel phoneme in a syllable (the *c* in *cat,* the *ch* in *chat,* the *chr* in *chrome*). *175*

Open syllable A syllable that ends in a vowel phoneme (*play, blue*). *115*

Phoneme The smallest unit of sound which distinguishes one word from another. This program identifies 44 phonemes. *10*

Phoneme addition Attaching one or more phonemes to a word or word part (adding /t/ to /able/ to pronounce /table/). *16*

Phoneme deletion Removing one or more phonemes from a word or word part (removing /s/ from /stop/ to pronounce /top/). *16*

Phoneme substitution Deleting one or more phonemes from a word or word part, and then replacing the deleted phoneme(s) with one or more different phonemes (deleting the /t/ from /sat/ and replacing it with a /d/ to pronounce /sad/). *17*

Phonetics The science of speech sounds. *133*

Phonics The study of the relationships of the letter and letter combinations (the graphemes of the English language) in written words to the sounds they represent in spoken words. The study of phonics provides the content for developing skill in the decoding of visually unfamiliar words. *9*

Phonological awareness The ability to conceptualize speech as a sequence of phonemes (sounds), combined with the ability to consciously manipulate the phonemes of the English language. Children who are phonologically aware can separate words into their individual phonemes, add, subtract, substitute, and rearrange the phonemes in words, and blend phonemes together to pronounce words. *14*

Rime The vowel and consonant letter(s) which follows it in a syllable. There is only one vowel phoneme in a rime (the /ă/ in *at,* the /ō/ in *oat*). *177*

Schwa A vowel phoneme in an unaccented syllable which represents a soft "uh," and is indicated by the key symbol, ə, which resembles an inverted *e*. Key words: comma, chicken, family, button, circus. *122*

Segmentation The process of separating spoken words or syllables into their individual phonemes. *15*

Semantic cues The general meaning of a passage which gives the reader useful information for word identification. *21*

Short vowel The vowel letters *ă, ĕ, ĭ, ŏ,* and *ŭ* which, in the context of the teaching of phonics, are indicated with a breve (˘), and heard in the key words, *apple, elephant, igloo, ox,* and *umbrella*. *99*

Silent letter A name given to a letter that appears in a written word but is not heard in the spoken word: *knight* has six letters, but only three are sounded, *k, g,* and *h* are "silent." *35*

Slash marks Slanting lines / / enclosing a grapheme indicating that the reference is to its sound, not to the letters. *10*

Syllable The unit of pronunciation. The English syllable has only one vowel phoneme. There are as many syllables in a word as there are vowel phonemes; there is only one vowel phoneme in a syllable. *155*

Syntactic cues Information from the order of words in phrases, clauses, and sentences which also gives the reader useful information for the identification of visually unfamiliar words. *21*

Voiced th The initial phoneme heard in the key word *that* in which the vocal cords vibrate during the production of the phoneme. *78*

Voiceless th The initial phoneme heard in the key word *thumb*, in which the vocal cords do not vibrate during the production of the phoneme. *78*

Vowel digraph A two-letter vowel grapheme which represents one sound. In this text, the vowel digraphs are the *o͞o* in *food* and the *o͝o* in *hook*. *136*

Vowel pair Two adjacent vowel letters that represent a phoneme associated with one of the letters, such as the /ā/ in *rain* which is represented by the *ai* grapheme. In this text, we use the term *vowel pair* to distinguish two-letter vowel graphemes that do not represent a distinct sound, that is, a sound that is not already represented by one of the vowel letters individually. *139*

Vowels One of the two classifications of speech sounds. The vowels are *a, e, i, o, u,* and sometimes *w* and *y*. (*See* Consonants.) *95*

Appendix A: Phonics Generalizations

Consonant Generalizations

1. Consonant letters are fairly reliable: There is a high relationship between the letter and the sound (/ /) we expect it to represent. p. 27. However, there are irregularities:

   a. A letter may represent more than one phoneme. p. 19
   Some common patterns are:

c: /k/, /s/	*n: /n/, /ng/*
d: /d/, /t/	*s: /s/, /sh/, /z/, /zh/*
g: /g/, /j/	*z: /z/, /s/, /zh/*

   b. A phoneme may be represented by more than one letter. p. 19
   Some common patterns are:

/f/: f, gh, ph	*/s/: s, z*
/j/: j, g, dg, d	*/w/: w, u*
/k/: k, ch, q	*/z/: z, s*

   c. A letter may represent no phoneme, that is, it may be silent. p. 19 When two like-consonants appear together, the second usually is silent. p. 39
   Some common silent letter patterns occurring in the same syllable are:

b following *m*	*k* followed by *n*
b followed by *t*	*l* followed by *m, k, d*
c following *s*	*p* followed by *s, t, n*
c followed by *k*	*t* following *f;* followed by *ch*
g followed by *n*	
h following *k, g, r,* following a vowel and as the initial letter in certain words	

2. When the letter *c* or *g* is followed by *e, i,* or *y,* it usually represents its soft sound as in *city* or *gem;* when *c* or *g* is followed by any other letter or

appears at the end of a word, it usually represents its hard sound as in *cup* or *go.* p. 57, 69

3. The suffix *ed* usually forms a separate syllable when it is preceded by *t* or *d.* When *ed* does not form a separate syllable, the *d* may represent /*t*/ or /*d*/. p. 46, 50
4. The letter *q* always represents /*k*/. p. 32, 41
5. The letters *c, q,* and *x* have no distinctive phonemes of their own. p. 29
6. The consonants *w* and *y* are positioned before the vowel in a syllable. The consonant *y* is never silent. p. 60, 69
7. We use two-letter combinations (digraphs) to represent the seven consonant phonemes not represented by single letters (*ch, sh, th̸, th, wh, zh, ng*). p. 50, 72, 85

Vowel Generalizations

1. A letter may represent more than one phoneme. p. 97
2. A phoneme may be represented by more than one vowel letter. p. 97
3. A letter may represent no phoneme; that is, it may be silent. p. 110, 141
4. When a one-syllable word or accented syllable contains two vowels, one of which is a final *e,* the first vowel usually represents its long sound and the final *e* is silent. p. 110, 111
5. A single vowel in an open accented syllable often represents its long sound. p. 117, 120
6. A single vowel in a closed accented syllable usually represents its short sound. p. 104, 106
7. When *i* is followed by *gh* or when *i* or *o* is followed by *ld,* the vowel usually represents its long sound. p. 117, 120
8. If the only vowel letter in a word or syllable is followed by *r,* the vowel sound will be affected by that *r.* p. 131, 132
9. If the only vowel in a word or syllable is an *a* followed by *l* or *w,* the sound of the *a* is usually that heard in *tall.* p. 131, 132
10. When two vowel letters appear together in a one-syllable word or in an accented syllable, the first vowel often represents its long sound and the second is silent. This holds true most often for *ai, oa, ee, ey, ay* combinations. p. 141, 143
11. The vowel *y* always follows the vowel or is the only vowel in a syllable and is silent or represents the phonemes we associate with *i* or *e.* p. 96
12. Although a syllable may have more than one vowel letter, there is only one vowel phoneme in a syllable. p. 155

13. The vowel phoneme is the most prominent part of the syllable. p. 157
14. Vowels behave differently in accented and unaccented syllables. The vowel is most clearly heard in the accented syllable. p. 117, 157
15. The vowel in most unaccented syllables represents the ə or *ĭ* p. 123, 125

Accent Clues

1. When a word contains a prefix and/or a suffix, the accent usually falls on or within the root word. p. 158, 162
2. The accent usually falls on or within the first word of a compound word. p. 159, 162
3. In a two-syllable word that functions as either a noun or a verb, the accent is usually on the first syllable when the word functions as a noun and on the second syllable when the word functions as a verb. p. 159, 162
4. When there is a double consonant within a word, the accent usually falls on the syllable that ends with the first letter of the double consonant. p. 159, 162
5. In multisyllabic words ending in *tion,* the primary accent falls on the syllable preceding the *tion* ending. p. 160, 162
6. When the vowel phoneme within the last syllable of a two-syllable word is composed of two vowel letters, that syllable is usually accented. p. 159, 162
7. When there is no other clue in a two-syllable word, the accent most often falls on the first syllable. p. 159, 162

Syllabic Division

1. In a compound word, the syllabic division usually comes between the words of which it is composed. p. 159
2. Prefixes and suffixes usually form separate syllables from the root word. p. 169, 172
3. If the last syllable of a word ends in *le* preceded by a consonant, that consonant usually begins the last syllable. p. 170, 172
4. If the first vowel in a two-syllable word is followed by a single consonant, that consonant often begins the second syllable. p. 165, 167, 172
5. When two vowel letters are separated by two consonants, the syllabic division usually occurs between the consonants. p. 166, 172
6. In syllabication, digraphs are treated as representing single phonemes. p. 168, 172

Appendix B:

Graphemes, Key Symbols, and Key Words

Grapheme	Key Symbol	Key Word
Single Consonants		
b	b	boat
c	no key symbol	no key word
d	d	dog
f	f	fish
g	g	goat
h	h	hat
j	j	jeep
k	k	kite
l	l	lion
m	m	moon
n	n	nut
p	p	pig
q	no key symbol	no key word
r	r	ring
s	s	sun
t	t	table
v	v	van
w	w	wagon
x	no key symbol	no key word
y	y	yo-yo
z	z	zipper

Grapheme	Key Symbol	Key Word
Long Vowels		
a	ā	apron
e	ē	eraser
i	ī	ice
o	ō	overalls
u	ū	unicorn
Schwa (Vowels in Unaccented Syllables)		
a	ə	comma
e	ə	chicken
i	ə	family
o	ə	button
u	ə	circus
Other Single Vowels		
a	â	care
u	û	fur
a	ä	father
a	ô	ball

Grapheme	Key Symbol	Key Word
Consonant Digraphs		
ch	ch	chair
sh	sh	shoe
th	th	thumb
th	t̸h	that
wh	wh	whale
	zh	treasure
ng	ŋ	king
Short Vowels		
a	ă	apple
e	ĕ	elephant
i	ĭ	igloo
o	ŏ	ox
u	ŭ	umbrella
Diphthongs		
oi, oy	oi	oil
ou, ow	ou	house
Digraphs		
oo	o͞o	food
oo	o͝o	hook
Vowel Pairs		
ai (rain)	ā	apron
ay (play)	ā	apron
ea (each)	ē	eraser
ee (keep)	ē	eraser
oa (boat)	ō	overalls